Maritime Provinces

OFF THE BEATEN PATH™

OFF THE BEATEN PATH SERIES

Maritime Provinces

TRUDY FONG

A Voyager Book

The Globe Pequot Press

Old Saybrook, Connecticut

Copyright © 1996 by The Globe Pequot Press, Inc.

All rights reserved. No part of this book may be reproduced or transmitted in any form by any means, electronic or mechanical, including photocopying and recording, or by any information storage and retrieval system, except as may be expressly permitted by the 1976 Copyright Act or by the publisher. Requests for permission should be made in writing to The Globe Pequot Press, P.O. Box 833, Old Saybrook, Connecticut 06475.

Cover map copyright © DeLorme Mapping
Illustrations by Carole Drong

Off the Beaten Path is a trademark of The Globe Pequot Press, Inc.

Library of Congress Cataloging-in-Publication Data

Fong, Trudy.
    Maritime Provinces: off the beaten path / Trudy Fong. — 1st ed.
            p.   cm. — (Off the beaten path series)
    "A voyager book."
    Includes index.
    ISBN 1-56440-852-3
    1. Maritime, Provinces—Guidebooks.   I. Title.
F1035.8.F57   1996
917.1504'4—dc20   95-44789
                                                                            CIP

Manufactured in the United States of America
First Edition/First Printing

To Greg, companion of all my significant voyages—
"The only railroad romance that ever lasted."

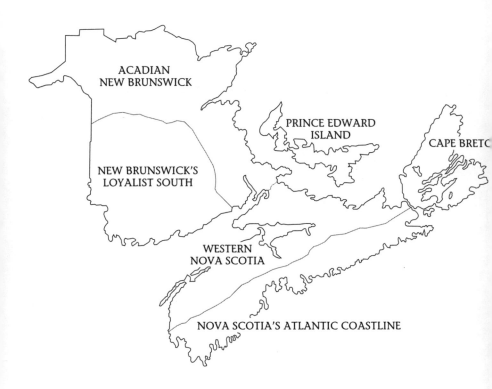

ACADIAN
NEW BRUNSWICK

PRINCE EDWARD
ISLAND

CAPE BRETO

NEW BRUNSWICK'S
LOYALIST SOUTH

WESTERN
NOVA SCOTIA

NOVA SCOTIA'S ATLANTIC COASTLINE

**MARITIME
PROVINCES**

CONTENTS

Introduction ix

New Brunswick's Loyalist South 1

Acadian New Brunswick.................................. 21

Prince Edward Island..................................... 41

Nova Scotia's Atlantic Coastline.......................... 77

Western Nova Scotia 105

Cape Breton.. 137

Index 169

ACKNOWLEDGMENTS

The following people have been wonderfully enthusiastic and informative and have inspired me with their special love of the Maritimes. I wish to thank them. Eleanor Mullendor, Lida Babineau and Ronnie Doucet, Helen Sievers, Cathy McDonald, Randy Brooks, Carol Horne, Valerie Kidney, Doug Fawthrop, Bob Benson, Ann Godard, Margaret and Axel Begner, Nora Parker, Webb Burns, Alida Visbach, Simone Larade.

All but one of the renderings in this book are drawn from photographs shot by my husband, photographer Greg Fong. The shot of the *Bluenose* II was supplied by the Nova Scotia Department of Economic Renewal.

INTRODUCTION

My first real experience of travel in the Maritimes came as a result of a job on Via Rail, the passenger-train service, which at that time left twice daily for Montreal from Halifax. I had graduated from college and was at loose ends when I took the job.

There were many opportunities to become familiar with the lay of the land as the train trundled by farms and woodlands, lakes and rivers. And with every stop the cultural and linguistic fabric would subtly change. Then as now, what struck me is the region's tremendous diversity, the vastness of the land, and the tiny communities that live in relative isolation from one another. Perhaps it is this isolation that has created fiercely independent peoples who are nevertheless able to extend exceptionally warm welcomes to outsiders. While exchange rates fluctuate and prices change, businesses close, and new spots open, there is an enduring quality about the Maritimes that keeps visitors coming back year after year.

If you are coming from another country, you will want to know just what your currency is worth compared to the Canadian dollar. To calculate conversions quickly, divide any Canadian price by the rate posted for your currency on that day.

Canada uses metric measurements for weight, distance, and temperature. Here I list measures according to the U.S. standards and provide their metric equivalents in parentheses. Take note that all road signs in Canada are in kilometers, not miles. Posted speed limits of 100, often shown without a "km," are really only 62 miles per hour.

Dressing for weather conditions in the Maritimes means packing layers. Carry a windbreaker, which is good in fog or mist; fog comes in the Maritimes about as often as the tides. A warm sweater is a good item to pack even in the summer months, because Maritime temperatures often drop significantly at night. Sunblock is also a must. The cool sea breeze or overcast skies can fool you into thinking that the sun is not very strong, but even a hazy day at the beach can result in a severe burn if you don't take precautions.

I include several good hikes in each province. These were selected for the natural wonders that you may discover along the trails, more than for their ease. That said, a good pair of walking shoes or, better still, hiking boots is a must. Hats are also a good idea, as is bug repellent in the countryside, particularly in the spring.

There are several levels of tax on consumption in Canada, which takes some getting used to. At press time the Goods and Services Tax, or GST, was 7 percent in all provinces. The provincial sales taxes hover around the 11 percent mark and are applied to the post-GST price. So even if an entree, a salad, and a dessert add up to a small restaurant bill, consider that you're then going to be paying close to 20 percent more in taxes plus a tip.

The good news is that visitors from outside the country can get a rebate on the GST by retaining their sales receipts and filling out a form that can be obtained at all provincial tourist information centers throughout the three provinces or at the Woodstock GST rebate center, located in the New Brunswick Duty-Free shop. (In Woodstock the rebate is instant, elsewhere you have to wait for the mail.)

Note that you can receive tax rebates only on items meant for consumption outside of Canada.

Most museum admission prices in the Maritimes are quite reasonable, since many of these sites are government-operated.

Accommodations under $70 are listed as standard: those priced from $70 to $150 are listed as moderate: and those over $150 are deluxe. In some remote areas the options are quite limited, so I have listed several places so that you can reserve ahead of time to avoid a last-minute search for a room. Remember that taxes are applied to the cost of accommodations. In a number of places I refer to Heritage properties. These are buildings or areas that various government bodies have determined to have significant historical connections. Having survived the plow and wrecking ball thus far, they have been designated by the government for future protection. Heritage properties are taxed at special rates, and the owners are assisted in restoration so that the sites may bee preserved for future generations. The "Heritage" designation means that the property is preserved as much as possible in its original state. Scenic Heritage Roads on Prince Edward Island are old clay roads that appear exactly as they did one hundred years ago and offer the traveler an abundance of scenic beauty.

Every trip has to start somewhere. That said, my travel throughout the Maritimes seems to have happened consistently in a clockwise direction. Therefore, if your entry point into the Maritimes is not the same as the beginning of this guidebook, merely search through the index for your starting point and follow the route clockwise from that point onward.

The Maritimes are full of hidden treasures, for the gourmet, the photography buff, or the artist. This book is intended as a compass, to help you make your own personal discovery of the wonders that Canada's east coast has to offer. *Bon voyage!*

The prices and rates listed in this guidebook were confirmed at press time. We recommend, however, that you call establishments before traveling to obtain current information.

NEW BRUNSWICK'S LOYALIST SOUTH

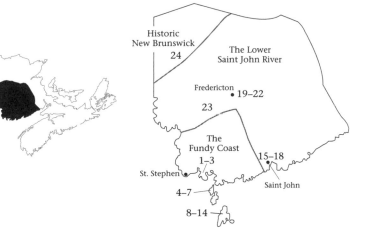

Historic New Brunswick
24

The Lower Saint John River

Fredericton • 19–22

23

The Fundy Coast
1–3

St. Stephen •

15–18

Saint John

4–7

8–14

1. Minister's Island
2. Rossmount Inn
3. Learn to Sail course
4. Deer Island Point Park
5. Old Sow
6. Roosevelt Cottage
7. Roosevelt Campobello International Park
8. Grand Manan Island
9. Hole in the Wall
10. Compass Rose / Aristotle's Lantern
11. Artist's Workshop
12. Machias Seal Island
13. Anchorage Provincial Park
14. Seal Cove
15. Dufferin Inn / San Martello Dining Room
16. Carlton Martello Tower
17. City Market
18. Irving Nature Park
19. York–Sunbury Historical Society Museum
20. Beaverbrook Art Gallery
21. Legislative Assembly Building
22. Christ Church Cathedral
23. King's Landing Historical Settlement
24. Hartland / World's longest covered bridge

NEW BRUNSWICK'S LOYALIST SOUTH

The first province you reach when entering the Maritimes by land is New Brunswick, with its vast, unpopulated interior full of rich timberlands and salmon rivers.

The first characteristic that will strike one is that the bulk of the population is distributed around the rim of the province. Next, you will notice that the province retains many native Indian place names, but certain areas, like the northwestern interior and the gulf coast, have a preponderance of French names, while the Fundy coast and the St. John River Valley feature many names with their origins in Great Britain.

These are clues to the character of New Brunswick. Overlaid on a land inhabited by people of the Maliseet and Micmac tribes for thousands of years, today the province's linguistic fabric resembles that of Canada as a whole more closely than any other province: Roughly 34 percent of the population are French-speaking, with the remainder using English in their day-to-day communication.

New Brunswick is really two places in one: the French New Brunswick of the northwest and the north and east coasts, and the British Empire Loyalist New Brunswick of the St. John River Valley and the Fundy shore. It is because of these two distinct characters, rather than any particular geographical reason, that we discuss New Brunswick in two separate chapters. The first, the Loyalist South, begins at the Maine–New Brunswick border, where Yankees and British Loyalists have lived cheek-by-jowl for two centuries.

THE FUNDY COAST

If you enter New Brunswick from Calais, Maine, you're struck by the fact that the national border runs right smack dab through the middle of town. In fact, Calais and **St. Stephen** natives have had such congenial relations that they refused to fight each other during the War of 1812. They still seem to form one community.

Follow the TransCanada Highway (TCH) Route 1 to **St. Andrews-by-the-Sea.** The signs will indicate St. Andrews long before anything much appears: the town is there, hidden behind trees. Watch carefully for the sign indicating Provincial Highway 127. Turn right here and drive toward the shore.

You will soon see a small sign pointing left and indicating ⚑ **Minister's Island,** where you can visit the former **estate of Sir William Van Horne,** the builder of the Canadian Pacific Railway.

Take the left turn, then turn right onto Mowat Drive, and take another left onto the Bar Road. This will lead you to a barricaded bit of shoreline. A chart listing the times when people can visit the island is displayed there. In this area of the Bay of Fundy, the tides change the water level by about 25 feet. At high tide, the island is inaccessible by car, but at low tide a sandbar serves as the tail end of the Bar Road.

A small sign indicates the times when guides will lead small contingents of cars to the island. Wait here rather than crossing the bar to the island on your own—without a guide, a barricade will prevent you from entering even during low tide.

When you first arrive on Minister's Island, you will see a small stone building, then a windmill and a massive barn— in fact, one of the largest in Canada. It was here that Van Horne kept his prized herd of Dutch cattle and his thoroughbred horses.

Everything about William Van Horne was meticulous. Not only did he have the entire milking area washed—along with every cow—after each and every milking, but he also ordered a fresh layer of sawdust to be put down in the barn every night. To complete the task, the farmhands had to draw a Van Horne coat of arms in the sawdust! The barn also has a lovely old carriage, which looks like it is still awaiting horse and driver.

Van Horne had his country house built on the other side of the island, using sandstone cut from the shore. Its massive rooms are full of mahogany paneling and post-and-beam supports. The drawing room alone is as large as the average modern bungalow. There are fifty rooms in the house; seventeen of these were bedrooms. In the billiards room is a 6-by 12-foot billiards table crafted for Van Horne in London.

Van Horne was an avid and skilled painter. Some of his finest paintings hang in the National Art Gallery in Ottawa. He created them at night in a huge, circular stone bathhouse overlooking Passamaquoddy Bay. A massive lamp was hung from the ceiling to illuminate his work. The property included several heated greenhouses. Van Horne's eight gardeners were able to produce peaches weighing as much as two pounds each. Even when Van

3

Carriage at Van Horne Estate

Horne lived in Montreal, the dairy products and fruit from his estate were sent via the Bar Road to a waiting train, to be delivered the next morning to him.

Sadly, after Van Horne's daughter died in 1941, the property remained empty for many years until it was sold to a succession of speculators, all of whose plans to turn it into a lodge fell through. More than 600 pieces of Van Horne's original mahogany furniture were auctioned off by one group of investors just three days before the province declared it a protected historic site. Even though today the building is emptied of nearly all its furnishings, it is still an amazing place and well worth checking the tide tables to visit.

After leaving Minister's Island, return to Highway 127 and drive east (in the direction of Saint John) for a few minutes. To your left will be a sign indicating the ◆ **Rossmount Inn.** Even if you don't stay here, plan to drop by to eat something so that you can soak up some of the Old World atmosphere inside.

There are so many pieces of pure Anglophile magic here that you'll swear you are in a manor house in England. In the front hallway, rich with mahogany paneling, banisters, and stairway and carpeted with Persian rugs, is a chair used by the King of Belgium during the Queen of England's coronation in 1952. The tables in the dining room are decked out in the finest English bone china and silverware, while the lamps are Tiffany. Reservations can be made by calling (506) 529–3351 or faxing (506) 529–1920. Rates are moderate.

This part of New Brunswick has long been the haunt of Ivy League types, who sail all summer long from one island to the next. Franklin D. Roosevelt learned to sail in this area. The waters of the bay are quite calm, and the islands are each quite unique and appealing.

If you want to try your hand at sailing here, you can sign up for a two-day intensive ✦ **Learn to Sail** course, taught on a 27-foot racing/cruising yacht. You need to reserve a spot at the sailing school at least a week in advance. The twelve-hour course allows you to sail in sheltered Passamaquoddy Bay, amid seals and porpoises. Students stay in a three-star historic (1884) bed and breakfast and have plenty of time to putter around the old town of St. Andrews. The B&B supplies two boxed or picnic lunches and two hot full breakfasts per person.

From mid-May to mid-June, and from the end of the first week in September to the end of the first week of October the cost, including lodging, is $177 per person. During the summer months the price rises to $198. For more details, contact Chamcook Forest Lodge/Prince Yacht Charter Ltd. at RR #2, St. Andrews-by-the-Sea, New Brunswick E0G 2X0. The phone number is (506) 529–4778 or (506) 529–4185.

Now that you are in New Brunswick, you may as well check out some of the seventy-odd "kissing bridges," or covered wooden bridges that span the many woodland rivers, particularly on old logging roads. While picturesque, they can be quite tricky to find without detailed directions. The best approach is to work in a visit to a couple of bridges en route to somewhere else, with a slight detour onto a secondary road that will take you near a bridge.

5

The purpose of covering bridges was to keep them from wearing out too soon. Uncovered wooden bridges last an average of ten years; covered ones last eight times as long. Surprisingly, it's not the snow that does the damage, but the sun and rain. It is because of the romantic opportunities they offered that they came to be called "kissing bridges." Crossing the bridges by horse and buggy or horse-drawn sleigh (in winter they were covered with snow so that sleighs could pass through) must have taken some time. If the horse was experienced and reliable, a romantic young couple could leave the driving to their four-legged friend and take advantage of the momentary privacy and darkness afforded by the covered bridges.

Among these seventy bridges is the so-called **covered bridge Number Four,** which spans the Digdeguash River, near McCann. You can reach it by turning off Route 127 onto Route 770.

The next stop is **Deer Island,** which is reached by the Deer Island L'Etete Ferry, off Route 1 at St. George. Take Route 772. Departures are frequent, and the ferry is free. The crossing takes about twenty-five minutes and is quite pleasant, especially on a sunny day when a cool breeze is blowing across the calm waters of Passamaquoddy Bay. The ferry lands at Lambert's Cove.

On Deer Island, take the left fork in the road. This will take you past Richardson, where you can join a **Cline Marine, Inc.** boat for a whale-watching cruise. For information, call (506) 529–4188 or (506) 747–2287.

After Richardson, continue to follow the shore road until you reach the Eastport/Campobello Ferry dock just before the ✦ **Deer Island Point Park.** If you have timed the tides right, enter the park to get a close-up view of ✦ **Old Sow,** the biggest natural tidal whirlpool in the Western Hemisphere, in the water just offshore, opposite the Deer Island Point Park campground, to the right of the dock.

You must be on site three hours before high tide to see Old Sow do its thing. If you are too early, relax and await the forces of nature at the picnic area here at the park.

The ferry ride from Deer Island to **Campobello Island** takes 45 minutes. It's privately run, so expect to pay $11 for a car and driver plus a fee for every passenger in your vehicle. Campobello is beautifully located on the Bay of Fundy. It's easy to see how it grew into a summer retreat for yachtsmen and Harvard grads.

If you desperately want to drive to Campobello Island through the United States but are in Canada, point your Pontiac south for the Maine border and get onto State Highway 1 from Calais, heading south in the direction of Machias. When you get to Whiting, turn left and head to Lubec on Route 189. In all, you'll drive about 50 miles on highways south of the border. A round-trip by land involves two border crossings, with possibly time-consuming customs inspections—one to get out of St. Stephen and into Calais, another to pass from Lubec to Campobello. You may want to take the boat to the island and drive back or vice versa, so that you can see the lay of the land but not take up so much time as a round-trip drive.

You can also visit Campobello by boat. Cline Marine of Deer Island makes regular stops here during its whale-watching outings.

After passing through customs into Campobello Island, take Route 774 and continue along for 1.4 miles (2.4 km). Here you will find ◆ **Roosevelt Cottage,** one of a complex of several cottages that now are often used for conferences and meetings. Clustered next to one another facing Lubec, Maine, across the water, the cottages and surrounding acreage are part of the ◆ **Roosevelt Campobello International Park.**

Franklin D. Roosevelt spent many summers here. This is where he learned how to sail before he came down with polio at age thirty-nine. He eventually moved into a bedroom downstairs, just down the hall from his office. Everything in the house has been kept just as it was the last time Eleanor Roosevelt visited the cottage, right down to two massive megaphones left standing in the entrance to the dining room. (They were used to call the children in to eat.) Along with other memorabilia, you can see the flags presented to Roosevelt when he won the presidency. They now flank his desk.

Be sure to visit the house to the right of Roosevelt Cottage, which is part of the same complex. Graced with a roomy wrap-around sunporch made from logs, its living room's oval-shaped picture window treat visitors to a perfectly composed view of Lubec across the water. For details on Roosevelt Campobello International Park, call (506) 752-2922.

Also on the island you will find Herring Cove Provincial Park. It has a beach where you can enjoy the bracing water of the Bay of Fundy. The park also encompasses an active beaver pond and some breathtaking cliffs overlooking the sea. For information on

Roosevelt Cottage, Campobello Island

the Herring Cove Provincial Park, call (506) 752–2396. The park is on Route 774.

Before you leave Campobello Island, take advantage of the handy **Provincial Tourist Information Bureau,** which can book accommodations for you in other parts of the province at no charge. It is recommended that those planning to go on to nearby ✤ **Grand Manan Island** take the time to book a room while still on Campobello. Campobello Island's tourist information center is just inside the Canadian border, next to Canadian customs, just a stone's throw from the bridge to Lubec, Maine. Open seasonally, it can be reached by phone at (506) 752–7043.

If you are in the mood to visit a remote, unspoiled place, **Grand Manan Island** is the ticket, but you can't easily get there from Campobello. The best route is via the ferry, which leaves from Blacks Harbour, southwest of Saint John. Sailings are frequent, and you pay only to get off Grand Manan, not on it; the cost is about $25.00 for a car and $8.00 more for the driver and each adult passenger. Children aged five through twelve pay half fare; children under five ride at no charge.

At the junction of Routes 785 and 776 on the mainland, take a right. Within five minutes you'll approach the ferry. Plan to take your car, since Grand Manan is quite large. The trip to Grand Manan is lengthy—roughly one and a half hours—and on breezy days you'll need either your sea legs or Gravol or both, because Grand Manan is all by its lonesome out in the Bay of Fundy, and the seas can be much rougher than landlubbers expect of a bay. (On the ferry are pictures of the vessel being tossed so wildly by the seas that one end or the other is completely out of the water.)

The ferry docks in **North Head.** If you get there before noon on a Saturday, you can visit the island's **farmer's market,** which is about 0.5 mile (1 km) from the ferry dock. For details and information on the Grand Manan Island ferry, call (506) 662–3724.

North Head is also the best place to get a look at the remains of the phenomenon that caused the island to come into being in the first place. Somewhere around 380,000 years ago, the ground folded up and formed the island out of a massive igneous rock. At North Head you can still see where the folding happened if you take the hike that begins at North Head's pier. It is marked by an incredibly understated sign announcing ✦ **Hole in the Wall** and indicating a pathway. This path leads to a rocky stretch of coast where the highlight is a rock formation with a massive hole in it. The hike is roughly 2 miles (3 km) long and takes about an hour round-trip.

Turning left off the ferry dock, proceed down Route 776. You will almost immediately spot a number of pretty little houses that have been converted to bed-and-breakfast establishments. There are two of note: **Compass Rose,** which offers a good view of the wharf and tiny North Head fleet; and, a short way up a lane directly across the street, **Aristotle's Lantern.**

In addition to accomodations, Compass Rose has generously packed lobster rolls, served up on fresh home-baked rolls. Note the local paintings on the walls of this establishment; many of them are framed in sea-weathered old planks and bits of driftwood. This type of framing is very characteristic of Grand Manan's artists. One such frame trims a lobster still life at

9

Compass Rose, which was painted for the previous owner as partial payment for a room.

Since Grand Manan is such a picturesque island, complete with quaint fishing communities, stunning sea vistas, lighthouses, and a bird sanctuary, it is a magnet for artists. You can get a good gander at their masterpieces, which are for sale at the ◆ **Artists' Workshop** at Aristotle's Lantern. This shop and the bed and breakfast are run by artist Helen Charters, whose paintings adorn every bit of open space on the walls and are stacked in bunches all over the place. She also sells carvings by her daughter, who creates *netsuke*-likemasterpieces on whales' teeth, bits of ivory, and even mastodon bone.

Helen also teaches small groups of three or four students for two-hour painting sessions in the mornings by arrangement; the fee is $20 per person per day. She says that after a week's training, the student's work will be good enough to sell.

For more information call (506) 662–3788 or write Helen Charters at P.O. Box 208, North Head, Grand Manan, N.B. E0G 1X0. Aristotle's Lantern's accommodations are priced inexpensively at standard rates, which refers to a typical range of up to $70 per night for a single room and a full breakfast.

Another art workshop in North Head, **Island Arts,** offers week-long programs throughout the summer in everything from porcelain to beach pottery to watercolor and oil painting.

Isolated as it is, there are a number of pleasant places to stay on the island, but you put yourself at risk if you do not reserve a spot before your arrival. The poshest digs on Grand Manan are in North Head, at the **Manan Island Inn and Spa,** which has a three-star Canada Select rating. Rates are standard. Call ahead to reserve a room at (506) 662–8624.

This area of North America's east coast is located on the migratory path of many species of birds, and the island's isolation has ensured their continued presence here. One of the neighboring islands is ◆ **Machias Seal Island,** a bird sanctuary. The island is home to puffins (which look like penguins in casual attire), razorbill auks, arctic terns, and other birds.

From mid-June through the first week of August, you can take a guided tour to the island and watch the puffins being their adorable selves from an arm's length away, since you will be concealed behind blinds. You can arrange this trip through your place of lodging, but be sure to do so well in advance, because only a limited number of people are allowed on the island.

There are five **lighthouses** on Grand Manan, pictures of which show up on scenic calendars with impressive regularity. It's easy to see why: Every corner of Grand Manan seems like a promontory at the end of the known universe, and land's end seems to be around every corner. Check out **Swallowtail Lighthouse** in particular if you want to get a feel for the rugged isolation of the island.

Grand Manan has two provincial parks, both along Route 776. The park in **Castalia** includes a picnic and rest area. Farther along Route 776, take the second left turn after the community of Grand Harbour to visit ✦ **Anchorage Provincial Park.** Here you can hike, recreate, or take advantage of the camping facilities, including fully serviced sites. For information on both parks, call (506) 662–3215.

Anchorage Provincial Park is just a stone's throw from ✦ **Seal Cove,** which is reached by taking the left turn off Route 776 after the park. Seal Cove, at the southern tip of the island, is a photographer's dream. Once in the village turn left and follow the signs to the breakwater to get some beautiful shots. (Plan to arrive with lots of film as there isn't much chance of stocking up in Seal Cove.) Viewed from the water's edge, Seal Cove is dotted with well-tended, neatly shingled and painted herring-smoking facilities. They look like a new cottage development. To the left of the smokehouses is a pleasant beach for strolling, beachcombing, or swimming.

At Seal Cove you can join a group of whale watchers with **Sea-watch,** a company operating from the southernmost pier in the village. To get there, stop next to the two churches of the community and turn onto the road directly opposite. Following this lane will take you up to the last pier of the cove. To book ahead with Seawatch call (506) 662–8552. Three other boat companies operate out of Grand Manan. They are **Island Coast Boat Tours** (506–662–8181); **Ocean Search** (506–662–8488); and **Starboard Tours** (506–662–8545 or (506) 633–7525).

THE LOWER SAINT JOHN RIVER

Back on the mainland, take Provincial Highway 776 until you reach the turnoff for the TransCanada. Head east on Route 1 to Lepreau and then take Highway 790 west toward the town of

Saint John, which lies at the mouth of the great Saint John River.

When you reach the Little Lepreau Road, you can take a slight detour to get a gander at the **covered bridge** on Little Lepreau River, overlooking a millpond. This road is closed to motor-vehicle traffic but is wonderfully scenic.

Saint John is a good place for antiques hunting, since this is where the Loyalists did their shipbuilding. If you are eager to look at some pieces, then emulate the locals and scan the news-paper for auction notices.

In the days of wooden ships, mahogany was prized because its density made it ideal as a ballast in the hull of the ships. Ship-builders would discard their mahogany "scraps," which furni-ture builders quickly gathered up to use in the making of furniture. Now that mahogany is so valuable, their work is quite a find.

You might want to stay at a Heritage inn in Saint John to enjoy many old-fashioned antique niceties, like four-poster beds and huge mahogany chests of drawers, all in a charming inn that happens to be run by one of the province's finest chefs. The ✦ **Dufferin Inn** and ✦ **San Martello Dining Room** are operated by Axel and Margaret Begner, who ran a hotel and restaurant in Germany for a decade. Axel, a European-trained master chef and pastry chef, has been cooking for twenty-five years. The restaurant is the sort recommended by other chefs; with dishes like stuffed baked pheasant, lamb ratatouille, and duck in a raspberry peppercorn sauce, you can be certain that you won't be bored with the selection.

The Begners came to Canada several years ago and renovated and restored the home of J. B. M. Baxter, a former premier and chief justice of the province. Be sure to visit the inn's library, where you will find a wealth of information on Saint John.

To get to the inn, travel to Saint John West on Route 109. Turn left onto Market Place just after crossing the bridge. Take a right turn onto St. John Street and continue along this street for five blocks, by which time the road will be called Dufferin Row. The inn is at 357 Dufferin Row. Room rates are moderate. Dinner runs about $40 per person for the set menu, plus wine and taxes.

The Dufferin Inn is just down the street from the ✦ **Carleton Martello Tower,** a stone battery built during the War of 1812.

Martello towers originated in the Mediterranean, where they were used as watchtowers. One such tower in Corsica allowed so stiff a resistance to its British attackers in 1793 and 1794 that the idea of using towers for coastal defense caught on in a big way. During the Napoleonic Wars, the British built more than a hundred Martello towers.

The flat roof of the Carleton Tower was meant to hold two twenty-four-pounder guns and two twenty-four-pounder carronades. It never was armed for the War of 1812—by the time the tower was finished, the war was over. The tower finally got some guns in 1866, when a group of Irish-American Fenians threatened to capture British North America in order to obtain Irish independence. Inside this particular tower you will see a barracks restored to the 1866 period, with the powder magazine restored to its 1840s appearance. For more information call (506) 636–4011.

While in Saint John you may want to visit the ❖ **City Market.** The building was constructed by famous shipbuilders, who also built one of the world's fastest sailing ships, the *Marco Polo*. The market has had a charter since 1785 (along with Saint John itself) and is the oldest farmer's market in Canada.

The City Market is a large, open space, made possible by the post-and-beam ceiling. Take a picture of this ceiling; when you get it developed, hold it upside down. Then you will see how the builders solved the problem of supporting a roof this size without a lot of braces: It's actually the upside- down hull of an old-time sailing ship!

The entrance to the market on Germain Street has been spiffed up to include a new glassed-in foyer and a spot for eating. The City Market is located at the corner of Charlotte and Germain streets. It is open year-round, except Sunday, from 8:30 A.M. to 5:30 P.M., Friday until 9:00 P.M. Admission is free.

If you proceed just past this market, you will soon come upon a park and then the old Loyalist graveyard, with markers dating back to the 1780s. The buildings along these streets and in the vicinity of Market Square are largely older buildings with intricate brickwork. You can hail a horse-drawn carriage to check out the downtown core if you want a different perspective.

Just outside of town, at the ❖ **Irving Nature Park,** you'll see harbor seals frolic at a location where 240 different species of birds have been spotted. To get there, take exit 107 off Route 1 onto Bleury Street, turn right on the Sand Cove Road, and drive 1.2 miles (2 km) to the park. For details call (506) 632–7777.

Now turn inland along the river valley to Welsford, on Route 7. Adjacent to Route 7, on the Cochran Road, about 1 mile (1.6 km) south of the community, you can admire a covered bridge over the Nerepis River. Then return to Route 101 north.

Inland on Route 101 you can see three more covered bridges without too much trouble. Exit Route 101 in Hoyt and turn onto Hoyt Station Road. There you will see Back Creek Bridge Number Two (Hoyt's Station).

Further along Route 101, turn off onto the Mill Settlement Road until you reach the North Mill Settlement Road—here you will find spanning the South Oromocto River another bridge called the South Oromocto Number Two (Mill Settlement).

Continuing on the Mill Settlement Road, you will come across the Boyne Road. At this point, turn right and continue until you reach the South Oromocto Number Three bridge, also called the Bell Bridge. From the Boyne Road, return to Route 101 and proceed toward the town of Fredericton.

Once you've puttered around historic **Fredericton,** walked under the city's many elms, and had a look at the many Victorian and Queen Anne homes, you will not find it at all surprising that many places here display the British flag. The United Empire Loyalists who came to New Brunswick left the same sort of indelible British stamp that one finds in former outposts of the empire like Belize, Malaysia's west coast, and India.

Fredericton is a wonderful town for strolling around, particularly because driving in the downtown is quite tricky. Many of the streets are one-way—with no prior indication until you come to an intersection and find youself facing the wrong way down a one-way street.

When you arrive in Fredericton, drop in first at the **City Hall** tourist office, which is right downtown on Queen Street (next to the water). Here you can get a tourist parking pass, available to any out-of-province vehicle for three days. This entitles you to park in the lot behind City Hall or at any meter without paying a cent or getting a ticket.

Turn left when you leave City Hall. You will soon come to the old garrison, now the ❂ **York-Sunbury Historical Society Museum.** Between this onetime officer's quarters and the guard-house is a parade ground in typical colonial British style, around which "soldiers" in period costumes march in traditional fashion.

A small fee is charged for admittance to the garrison museum, which houses a collection of artifacts associated with the early Loyalist pioneer days, from the early regimental ornamentation of colonial officers to memorabilia from the first World War. You can witness the changing of the guard several times a day here (all to the sound of bagpipes, so you will know it's starting from a long way off) from Tuesday to Saturday in July and August. The Officer's Square is also used for free evening concerts on Tuesday and Thursday during the summer months.

Just beyond the parade ground is a lighthouse-turned-giftshop, down on St. Anne Point. It has a large wooden deck where people can relax and enjoy the river views. In front of this is a charming riverfront walkway, **Waterloo Row.** On warm summer nights people stroll along the river while the odd houseboat and its occupants offshore look on. A number of speedboats tie up here, giving access to the downtown for people up- and downriver.

Proceeding in the same direction, away from City Hall, you will eventually come to a must-see attraction: the ◆ **Beaverbrook Art Gallery,** which has a huge painting by Salvador Dali and several other of his smaller works. The gallery has quite an extensive collection of art, including a number of paintings by Cornelius Krieghoff, J. M. Turner, John Constable, and Thomas Gainsborough. There are some works by the Group of Seven, Canada's most famous group of artists.

You will also find a number of Graham Sutherland studies of Winston Churchill. Commissioned by the British House of Lords and House of Commons, Sutherland's definitive portrait was presented to Churchill as an eightieth birthday gift. Both Sir Winston Churchill and Lady Churchill hated the portrait. After its presentation, it was never allowed to be seen again. Within a year Lady Churchill reportedly destroyed it. The gallery is at 703 Queen Street. Call (506) 458–8545 or (506) 458–8546.

The art gallery is named for William Maxwell Aitken, who became Lord Beaverbrook. He was born in Ontario but grew up in Newcastle (now Miramichi). He served in Britian as the minister of aircraft production during World War II, but his chief claim to fame is his becoming a "press baron" with the empire he created from *The Daily Express* newspaper. The name Beaverbrook is forever connected to the Fleet Street newspapers in England.

One other building you must get a look at before leaving Queen Street is the ✦ **Legislative Assembly Building,** the seat of the provincial government, which is across the street from the gallery. This particular colonial sandstone building dates from 1882, when it was constructed to replace an earlier edifice destroyed by fire. The whole structure, including its fittings and furnishings, cost $120,000 in the currency of the 1880s. (At that time, a typical annual salary was $300.) It is constructed in the 'Second Empire' style, with a mansard roof and corner towers.

There is no mistaking just which empire mattered when this was built. Perched like some daring stuntman in the exact center of the facade is a statue of Britannia with her trident. Other colonial reminders are inside: Portraits of King George III and Queen Charlotte flank the throne in the chamber. (The province was named after George III—when New Brunswick was separated from Nova Scotia in 1784, it was named for his family's ancestral seat, Brunswick in Germany.)

In this area of New Brunswick, the British Loyalists almost completely supplanted the Acadian settlers, and there is no stronger evidence of this than the city's old architecture.

Two blocks farther away from the water and a block east is ✦ **Christ Church Cathedral,** on Church Street. To get there on foot, follow Queen Street as it rounds the point for another block or so past the legislature building.

The outside masonry was recently touched up, so the cathedral should be at its most presentable when you visit. This is an impressive Gothic church, a copy of St. Mary's at Snettisham, England. The cornerstone was laid in 1845, with construction completed in eight years. This was the first entirely new cathedral foundation on British soil since the time of the Norman Conquest in 1066.

From mid-June until Labour Day, you may join a free guided tour of the cathedral on Monday to Friday from 9:00 A.M. to 8:00 P.M., and on Saturday from 10:00 A.M. to 5:00 P.M. Sunday visits are limited to the afternoon, from 1:00 P.M. to 5:00 P.M. For details call (506) 450–8500.

If you happen to be in Fredericton in mid-September to admire the glorious fall foliage of the "city of elms," you can enjoy the **Harvest Jazz and Blues Festival.** For specifics on this annual event, call (506) 454–2583.

16

A pleasant stand of virgin forest can be found at **Odell Park,** just outside the downtown core. Take Smythe Road headed away from the water and turn left just after Dundonald Street. You will then be at one end of the park, wedged between it and the Fredericton Exhibition Grounds. The park is quite extensive, so plan to spend at least a full morning or afternoon roaming around here.

There are beaches around here, including at Killarney Lake, 5 miles (8 km) from Fredericton on the Killarney Road. Fairly close by, a covered bridge spans the Keswick River, at Stone Ridge. It is roughly 4½ miles (4.8 km) off Route 104 on the Morehouse Road, going north from Fredericton.

If you are staying in Fredericton overnight, consider checking in at the **Carriage House Inn,** which is located on University Avenue, 2 blocks away from the Beaverbrook Gallery and the legislature. The home of a former mayor and lumber baron, the cozy inn is lovely mahogany Victorian. Rates are standard, i.e. up to $70 per night for a single room.

HISTORIC NEW BRUNSWICK

Twenty minutes' drive outside of Fredericton is a large **hydroelectric dam,** the building of which flooded a sizable chunk of woodland some thirty years ago. From the town, get on the TransCanada Highway Route 2 headed west, and turn off onto Provincial Highway 105 at the Mactaquack turnoff.

There is a beautiful park here with a good golf course and a warm beach along the edge of the lake created by the dam. The cost per vehicle entering the park is only $3.50 for the day. As you dip your toes in the lake consider this: The entire area was once a forest, submerged under the water now for thirty years. The buildings that used to be in here were moved to an area twenty minutes away: They became ◈ **King's Landing Historical Settlement.**

To get there from Mactaquack, return to Highway 105 and drive for a minute or two until you reach the turnoff for Trans-Canada Highway Route 2 turnoff. Head west in the direction of MacAdam. Fifteen minutes later a series of signs will direct you to King's Landing.

It's authentic right down to the cow pies in the field. One hundred costumed residents and more than sixty authentically restored buildings re-create a United Empire Loyalist settlement dating back to the days of the American War of Independence.

These living-history lessons are always lots of fun, but King's Landing is also quite historically accurate. The assistant curator told me that when the houses were moved to their new locations, they were even oriented in exactly the same way as they were in their previous site. That is, if they were built on a sloping hill with a kitchen in the basement, with one side of the lower floor exposed, that was exactly how it was set up on its new location.

Visitors leave their cars at the reception building and then walk along a dirt road to the old-time settlement, so no sign of the modern world is evident. A horse-drawn cart helps with the commute to the village; you'll see youngsters in costume hitching a ride on this cart, or weeding the gardens and doing other chores.

These young people are participants in a program that allows them to stay at the settlement for five days, living life exactly as it was lived in the previous century. The program, called "Visiting Cousins," takes kids from ages eight to twelve years, for a cost of just $50. A number of the participants have been here before, resulting in the extension of the program into different age categories. The historic re-creation has expanded to an elderhostel program as well as programs that allow day visitors to spend their time learning crafts and doing chores from the previous century. In each of the houses, female participants are required to cook meals for eight to fifteen people using methods from bygone days.

At the blacksmith shop you can watch a skilled craftsman turning out tools to be used in the settlement's other enterprises—hooks for holding logs at the sawmill, for example.

The cooper who I watched making wooden buckets has it down to a science, slowly carving out the perfect curve in each slat so that a group of them will result in a round, airtight bucket. Eight hours of work will give you a bucket worth forty cents, he notes—"A good day's pay."

The settlement includes a sawmill with the largest functioning waterwheel in Canada. I watched a log being maneuvered into position for cutting, a process that took a good half hour.

If you are interested in sampling some of the early settlers' home-style cooking, drop by the **King's Head Inn** for lunch. (There are also benches outside.) After lunch, hitch a ride on the horse-drawn cart outside the door of the inn back to the reception center.

For more details on the various programs, call (506) 363–5090 or fax (506) 363–5757; write to King's Landing Historical Settlement, Prince William, N.B. E0H 1S0.

Just after this settlement is **Lake George Provincial Park,** about 7 miles (11 km) off Route 2 west on Route 259, or 8 miles (13 km) north of Harvey on Route 636. There is a lovely beach here.

Whether you find yourself in Prince William, King's Landing, or Lake George, when you want to resume your travels, return to the TransCanada via Route 2 and drive northwest to Pokiok. It is about 13 miles (21 km) north of Prince William. From here you can cross the Saint John River (it's quite narrow at this point), turn right at the fork in the road at the end of the crossing, and proceed to Nackawic and then Millville, about 9½ miles (15 km) farther on.

Turn left onto Route 104, then left onto Route 585. To see the Nackawic Siding covered bridge that straddles the Nackawic River here, take the exit to Nortondale, just north of the main road. Then return to Route 585 and in about a half hour you will come to **Woodstock,** which is at most a 20-minute drive from the Canada-U.S. border. Woodstock is a pretty little town for stretching your legs (and for shopping when the currency exchange rate favors it).

Communities that straddle the border in this area are at the mercy of changing fiscal policies and monetary fluctuations, so businesspeople on both sides of the border find themselves suffering periodic downturns due to the drop in their neighbor's dollar.

To view yet another covered bridge, turn back onto Route 2 and head south toward Meductic. Just before Meductic you will see a sign for Benton. Turn right here and continue until you reach the Benton Village Road. Here, the covered Benton Bridge crosses the Eel River, which also serves as the county line for a while along its meandering path.

Now return to Route 2 and head north past Woodstock to ✦ **Hartland.** As if you haven't already seen enough of covered bridges, now you come to the granddaddy of them all, the **world's longest covered bridge,** at 1,282 feet (390.8 m) in length. Imagine the possibilities for clandestine romantic interludes presented by a kissing bridge that took a horse a good quarter hour to traverse. The bridge remains a popular site to this day, long after automotive breakdowns and drive-in movies replaced it as a lovers' hot spot. To the east of Hartland you will come to the Becaguimec River system and a collection of yet more picturesque covered bridges.

ACADIAN NEW BRUNSWICK

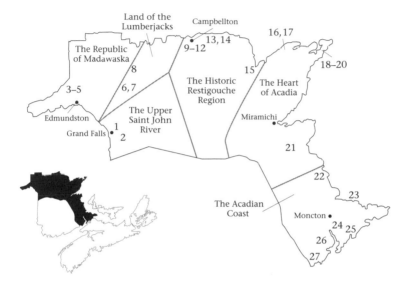

Land of the
Lumberjacks   Campbellton
13,14   16,17
The Republic   9–12
of Madawaska   18–20
8   15
3–5   6,7   The Historic   The Heart
Restigouche   of Acadia
Region
The Upper
Edmundston   Saint John   Miramichi
1   River
Grand Falls   2   21
22
23
The Acadian
Coast   Moncton
24 25
26
27

1. Grand Falls
2. New Denmark
3. New Brunswick
   Botanical Garden
4. Antique Automobile Museum
5. Petit-Temis
   Interprovincial Park
6. Centre Plein Air du Vieux
   Moulin
7. Kedgwick Outdoor
   Recreation Centre
8. Forestry Museum
9. Sugarloaf
10. Restigouche Sam
11. Train Station Museum
12. Gallery Restigouche

13. *Chaleur Phantom*
14. Eel River Sandbar
15. Daly Point Reserve
16. Acadian Historical Village
17. Musee de Cire d'Acadie
18. Ste.-Cecile International
    Festival of Baroque Music
19. Miscou Island Camping
20. Miscou Lighthouse
21. Kouchibouguac National Park
22. Ile-aux-Puces
23. Cap Pele Beach
24. Sackville Waterfowl Park
25. Fort Beausejour
26. Hopewell Cape
27. Fundy National Park

ACADIAN NEW BRUNSWICK

THE UPPER SAINT JOHN RIVER

As you drive inland along the Saint John River Valley, you will gradually enter the land that has been home to the Acadians for more than three hundred years, despite massive population upheavals. One historian noted that because of the great distance from the French capital at Port Royal, the Acadian French, who lived in these parts long before the British takeover in 1755, had no real force of law, and yet they managed to maintain societal order purely through their sense of community.

Once uprooted in 1755 from their homes, they were determined to return to this independent way of life, so much that many Acadians deposited along the Eastern Seaboard spent years finding their way back to Acadia, only to discover that their lands had been taken over by Englishmen. They then settled informally along the coast and in the northern interior of New Brunswick.

Without external structure or governmental endorsement, they managed to keep their language, traditions, and culture intact. They remained loyal to their identity even though the boundaries of Acadia could never be shown on a map.

The first major stop along Route 2 in Acadian New Brunswick is ♦ **Grand Falls,** noted for a set of gorges and a series of falls that step by step, descend a total of about a mile (1.6 km). If the weather has been dry, Grand Falls is not quite as spectacular as in rainy seasons. But, periodically the people who run the electrical generating station situated at the falls let a backlog of water go, so be sure to check when the gates are due to be released if you want to see the falls in their full glory.

The massive rockface through which the water flows is, in itself, quite something to see. At night it is illuminated with colored lights, making for a surreal spectacle.

An interpretive center at the power station has a scale model where tour guides explain exactly how the generator functions. Called the Malobiannah Information Centre, it is named for a young Malecite Indian maiden. According to Indian legend, the young girl was captured by Mohawks. Forced to head an expedition of Mohawks who intended to attack her village, the girl instead led all of them to their doom over the gorges of Grand Falls.

This is a region of fertile farmland. The biggest crop here is the potato, which New Brunswick produces more of than any other province in Canada. Grand Falls holds an annual potato festival and crowns a "Miss Potato" to preside over the festivities.

If you think that a small center like Grand Falls doesn't have nightlife, then think again. Indeed, it's noted for it in the region. The main drag in town is particularly wide, since it was used at one time for military parades. Once those kind of spectacles ended, the wide street was turned into a divided boulevard with a park running down the middle, complete with gazebo and a few of the old pieces of military hardware. On hot summer nights all of Grand Falls seems to show up, walking or driving down this street. Conversely, in winter it's cold in Grand Falls, and there are no real nightlife hot spots to warm lingering travelers.

If you are staying in the neighborhood for any length of time and are feeling a bit restless, drive from Route 2 to Route 108 and then on to ◆ **New Denmark.** (Note, however, that you must follow the signs for Plaster Rock, since New Denmark does not figure prominently on the maps.) This is a trek of 10 miles (16 km) on secondary road, but the scenery, provided in part by the lush potato farmlands and partially by the distant hills, is well worth the time and effort.

This is the site of Canada's first Danish settlement. The area was settled by Danes in 1872. They had been assured that it was good farmland, but they discovered after they arrived that it was woodland that had to be cleared by manual labor. The small **New Denmark Memorial Museum** recounts their story and displays a collection of century-old dolls and porcelain from Copenhagen. Next door you will find **Immigrant House,** which depicts the life of the early settlers.

Since the settlers were farmers who stayed in the area for many years without moving around, many residents of this area over age forty-five still speak Danish. As you drive along Route 108 you will note a sign for the Valhalla Restaurant, with an arrow pointing left, up a hill.

In legend, Valhalla is the place where fallen Vikings go to feast after their death. In this least likely of spots in Acadian New Brunswick, situated as it is just where English-speakers become Francophones, Valhalla Restaurant is also a good place to enjoy a traditional Scandinavian meal—snitchel, pickled red cabbage, Swedish meatballs, Danish beer.

The owner, Stanley Jensen, is a charming gentleman with striking blue eyes. He says that the restaurant and the community are visited by quite a number of Scandinavians every year. During the meal he dropped by the table in full Viking regalia, right down to a blond Leif Ericson beard and horned helmet. "You see a lot of these at Halloween around here," he noted.

THE REPUBLIC OF MADAWASKA

About 35 miles (57 km) northwest of Grand Falls on Route 2 is **Edmundston,** the commercial hub for this neck of the woods. Across the Upper Saint John River is Madawaska, Maine. The residents of these communities cross the border the way other people cross the street. The flow of workers in the lumbering and related industries has caused the area to develop a distinctive character of its own, regardless of which side of the border its occupants live on. This is the **Republique de Madawaska,** named for the river that flows from across the Quebec border and into the Upper Saint John River.

Here the Upper Saint John serves as a border between Canada and the United States. Not many people today realize that during the last century, there was considerable wrangling about where the border actually fell. When it came to this particular area, the line kept getting moved around so much that in 1827 one man by the name of John Baker erected a flag in protest and declared the land the American Republic of Madawaska.

The name has stuck, and the memory of John Baker lives on in the form of Baker Brook and **Lac Baker,** wedged in the tiny strip of land between Maine and Quebec. As for John Baker, he was sent to jail for treason. Today you can visit a park at Lac Baker, which has picnic facilities, a nice beach, and lots of water sports.

This area of New Brunswick has become a major gateway to New Brunswick from Quebec, Maine, and upstate New York. It is lush agricultural land that can get quite hot in summer. Combine these —a flow of visitors from all over the region and excellent growing conditions—and you have the ideal location for a botanical garden.

In **St.-Jacques,** just off TransCanada Highway Route 2 and only 6 miles (10 km) south of the Quebec border, and ten minutes' drive north of Edmundston is the ❖ **New Brunswick Botanical Garden,** opened in 1993. Over a meticulously groomed 17-acre (7-hectare) site is a garden planned by the expert consultants to the Montreal Botanical Garden, including noted landscape architect Michel Marceau.

Though it is a magnificent garden, it is young, with many of the trees still establishing themselves. This affords an opportunity to get a feel for the planning that went into it. Nature has been coaxed into submission here: Large boulders were rearranged and water pumped in to create a miniature waterfall in the style of Grand Falls, complete with gorges. There are also several ponds.

The garden features 850 rosebushes of more than 50 varieties. The gardens comprise more than 30,000 annuals, with a total of 75,000 plants arranged in nine separate gardens. A staff of twenty-five tends the grounds. Hidden under the shrubbery are small outdoor speakers that broadcast classical music (at low volume), of a type deemed appropriate for each particular garden.

Avid gardeners take note: Although the greenhouses are not open to the public, they open their doors to gardeners who make the request to look around. There are a snack bar and gift shop on site. A small admission is charged.

The parking lot for the Botanical Garden is directly behind the ❖ **Antique Automobile Museum.** Along with other unusual cars, here you can get a look at the Bricklin, a failed automobile design that enjoyed a brief heyday in the 1970s when New Brunswick's premier Richard Hatfield threw his support behind a would-be entrepreneur who briefly established his factory in the province.

This area is part of a provincial park called **Les Jardins de La Republique,** which has the usual recreational and camping facilities. Nearby is the ❖ **Petit-Témis Interprovincial Park,** which you can access from the Botanical Garden. This linear park is a cycle path 80 miles (130 km) long that takes bicyclists into Quebec, along the shores of Lake Temiscouata and the bank of the Madawaska River. The trail reaches the town of Cabano and then continues on to Rivière du Loup.

Back in your car, if you've gone as far north as St.-Jacques, you're going to have to return to the outskirts of Edmundston via Route 2 and continue on this same stretch of highway to **St.-Léonard.** Then you can get onto Trunk 17 and head to Kedgwick.

(From St.-Jacques to the St.-Léonard exit is 32 miles, or 56 km—not that much of a detour to see the beautiful Botanical Garden and cycle path.)

LAND OF THE LUMBERJACKS

Almost as soon as you leave St.-Léonard you'll be surrounded by dense forest, the trees so much alike that they appear to have been cloned from the same original seedling. In fact, these trees were planted at the same time after the area had been intensively logged.

The first large community after St.-Leonard is **St.-Quentin.** When a railway was built between St.-Léonard and Campbellton, this little community sprang up, named Five Fingers, after a brook of the same name. Then, after a logging company operating there caused the community to swell in size, it became Anderson Siding, named for the head of the Canadian National Railroad. (The "Siding" part of the name was common to any area where sawmills operated.) In 1919 the town was renamed again, this time to commemorate the Canadian victory in Saint-Quentin, France, during the world war.

The town's location in the middle of densely wooded New Brunswick seems incongruous with its chief claim to fame: St.-Quentin is home to the biggest annual Western festival in eastern Canada. Apparently, you can't get more country and western than St.-Quentin; even the streetlights are festooned with cowboy boots as the town puts its best foot forward for its mid-July shindig, culminating in a weekend-long rodeo including cowboys from the United States, western Canada, Quebec, and Ontario.

Here you can also rent canoes and go fishing or exploring the backwoods and rivers, at the ◆ **Centre Plein Air du Vieux Moulin.** For details and reservations call (506) 235–1110.

An interesting alternative is located near St.-Quentin. Leave Trunk 17 at the exit for Kedgwick River and take the smaller Collector Highway 265. It is here that you will find the rustic cabins of the ◆ **Kedgwick Outdoor Recreation Centre.** The facilities are of excellent quality, with some of the cabins large enough to accommodate up to eight people. For reservations call (506) 235–9088. Rates are deluxe.

If you don't detour to the Kedgwick River, you'll continue along Trunk 17 to **Kedgwick.** After you pass through what appears to be almost all of this community, you will see a sign marked MUSÉE FORESTIER. This is the ❖ **Forestry Museum,** formerly known as the "Heritage Lumbercamp." It provides a detailed look into the lives of lumberjacks before the introduction of modern tree-harvesting methods.

The complex includes a number of log cabins built under the direction of old-time loggers. The tour of the complex begins with a short film in which lumberjacks and storytellers recount their experiences in the woods from the last century to the 1960s. You will quickly see that the life of a lumberjack was extraordinarily hard. Your understanding of the logging industry will be

1937 Snowmobile at Kedgwick Forestry Museum

enhanced by the old tools and other artifacts that have been donated to the complex by people who worked in the industry.

Before you leave the camp, be sure to look at the 1937 snowmobile, the original item, the manufacture of which launched industrial giant Bombardier. It's a fascinating machine, fully enclosed and constructed of wood. And glance at the wall of the museum's main reception building. Here is mounted a forty-pound (19 kg) salmon, a fitting example of why the area is a favorite among anglers and outdoorsmen.

To resume your drive, continue along Trunk 17E.

THE HISTORIC RESTIGOUCHE REGION

Just before you reach Campbellton, you will see a turnoff for Madapédia Quebec. After this point be on the lookout for Atholville and one of the province's most popular ski slopes: ◆ **Sugarloaf.** Even if you are here in the summer, this slope is noteworthy: You can take the chairlift to the top and then slide down on a luge course made of cement. The view from the top of Sugarloaf is quite spectacular, well worth the $3.50 for the chairlift ride to the top.

Indian legend has it that Sugarloaf was once a massive beaver who was turned into the mountain by the Micmac god Glooscap. The beaver had angered the god by building a dam that prevented the salmon from swimming upriver to spawn. In anger, Glooscap destroyed the dam and turned the beaver into a ski hill. While he was at it, he cut the other beavers down to size, turning them into the small creatures they are today, as opposed to the mythic giants they once were.

Now continue on to **Campbellton.** It's a pretty little town, a gateway to Quebec. Just before the bridge across the river to Quebec, on the right-hand side, is a fountain, the centerpiece of which is a statue of a giant salmon, ◆ **Restigouche Sam,** promoted as "the largest salmon in the world." The fountain is surprisingly elegant, considering that it is dominated by a 28-foot (8.5 m) metal fish that appears to be in the throes of being reeled in by a giant angler.

The street where you will find this is Salmon Street. You can guess what the town's claim to fame is.

Campbellton has managed to maintain its rail connection, though many other communities in the region have lost theirs.

Restigouche Sam

The passenger service passes through six times a week, with its next stop Matapédia in Quebec. Railway lore abounds about the train from Halifax to Montreal and the many times that it literally was "frozen in its tracks." (You knew that expression had to come from somewhere!)

You can relive some of the old railway glory at the ◆ **Train Station Museum,** next door to the Tourist Information Centre, to the left of the exit to the bridge to Quebec. Outside the museum are an old locomotive and caboose in mint condition.

To the right of this turnoff, just down from the giant salmon fountain, is a lighthouse. This has been turned into a youth hostel. The lighthouse is small and not that interesting, but the hostel offers a rare opportunity to spend the night in a lighthouse. The doors are closed every day from noon until 4:00 P.M.

29

Just to the left of the Tourist Information Centre and to the right of the giant salmon fountain as you face the water is Andrew Street. The ◆**Gallery Restigouche,** easily found by looking for the rather large statues at the front, houses a collection of regional, national and international exhibitions year-round. To get to the gallery, drive eight blocks up Andrew Street from the harbor. The gallery is on your right.

Campbellton was once the site of a native village. Over the centuries the Restigouche natives were gradually pushed farther north. Today the Restigouche Nation live on the other side of the water, in Quebec.

Few people realize it, but the final battle in which the English gained control of Canada from the French was fought just off these shores in 1760.

After the Battle of the Plains of Abraham in 1759 when Quebec City fell, the navies of the two countries met just outside Campbellton (then Restigouche) at a point about 3 miles (5 km) east along Route 132, on the Quebec side of the border. It is now a **national historic site** designated by a humble marker that belies its significance. As you drive there, you pass through native lands, at Pointe-à–la-Croix. These are the Restigouche Micmac who used to live on the New Brunswick side of the bay.

It is a short drive from Campbellton to **Dalhousie.** Follow either TransCanada Highway Route 11, which bypasses Dalhousie itself, or Highway 134, which takes a more meandering route into Dalhousie and then back out to River Charlo, where it connects to Route 11 again. From this point they become one road, following the coast along the **Baie des Chaleurs.**

If you want to putter around the area of Dalhousie, try the ◆ *Chaleur Phantom,* which offers both nature cruises and scenic cruises, depending on the time of day. The 50-foot boat also does private charters. It operates from late May to the first week in October.

The morning nature cruises offer close-up looks at seals, an area where eagles nest, the occasional whale, and a multitude of bird life, including black cormorants. The afternoon cruise involves sightseeing such as trips to the Bon Ami rocks and possibly some points on the Quebec side, and Heron Island, which is now the home of thousands of birds, and was at one time the home of nineteen human families.

The cruise itineraries vary, so it's best to ask if your particular trip will take you to the sites you want to see. Adult tickets are $15 per person, couples $20, for three-hour morning cruises. Afternoon cruises are two and a half hours long and cost $10 to $15. Children ride for half fare. For details or to reserve a trip, call (506) 684-4722 or (506) 684-4219.

A ferry leaves Dalhousie for Miguasha on Quebec's Gaspé Peninsula. Look for the sign on Route 11. This provides a cheap alternative to the scenic cruise, which you can round off with a trip to the Miguasha Fossil Park. The ferry operates only in summer and leaves every half hour between 9:00 A.M. and 9:00 P.M. Fares are $2 for the driver and each passenger, plus $12 per vehicle.

Just outside of Dalhousie is a beach with the longest natural sandbar in North America. Blue herons fish inside it. Locals call it the ◆ **Eel River Sandbar** or Eel River Beach, but it's marked on the map as Charlo, which is apparently another beach that runs into the sandbar. To reach it you must get on Highway 380. This minor road connects to Highway 134 in a rather confusing way, so be sure you are headed east. Incidentally, as you drive from Dalhousie to Eel River Sandbar via Highway 134, you will be passing through a native community.

The day I dropped in to check out the Eel River Sandbar, the beach was the meeting place of 3,500 Boy Scouts from all over the region. (Apparently, there are a lot of scout camps in the vicinity.) A madhouse, you say? Near the food concession, perhaps, but the beach is sufficiently long that at the other end there wasn't a sign of a crowd.

The beach is a bit on the pebbly side, so beach sandals will come in handy. Several other pleasant beaches are along this coast. Most of them are not visible from the road, however, so you need to be armed with a map. Unlike Nova Scotia, where roads follow the coast, with lighthouses and beaches self-evident, roads in New Brunswick are almost always a bit of a way from the shore.

One beach that is not so hidden away is at Jacket River Park on Highway 134. The beach is accessible through a small provincial park, entrance to which costs a dollar per vehicle. **Fenderson Beach** is behind the campsite, down a small hill. The water here is quite shallow, and therefore warm enough for even the fussiest swimmers. From this point, on a clear day, you can see across the water to Quebec. The stretch of land up and down the coast from this point appears as unbroken wilderness.

31

The next major urban center is **Bathurst,** which you can reach by either TransCanada Highway Route 11 or Highway 134, the more scenic of the two; it also passes by several more beaches, but you won't get much of a look at them from the road). When you are there, be sure to visit the **Nicolas Denys Monument** on Main Street overlooking Bathurst Harbour.

This Nicolas Denys was quite a busy chap. In the 1650s he established a fur-trading post in the then virgin territory of Cape Breton (see pg. 166). When you visit Cape Breton, you'll see a small museum dedicated to and named for Denys along the side of the St. Peter's Canal. In Miscou you'll pick up Denys' traces, and here, somewhere in Bathurst's Gowan Brae Golf and Country Club, he is believed to be buried.

After his exploits in Cape Breton, this native of Tours, France, was made governor of the entire gulf region of New France, from Cape Breton to the Gaspé Region of Quebec. Denys wrote one of the first classic works on the people of Acadia, a century before the Expulsion, which uprooted them from their homes in Nova Scotia and left them scattered throughout the eastern seaboard.

Because of the instrumental role he played in bringing over settlers, Denys is credited with giving the region its distinctive Acadian flavor, with its mixed population of fishermen, fur traders, and farmers who were expert in farming the marshlands. (Many of the latter came from an area of France with the same kinds of marshlands, farmed for centuries by their ancestors.) In 1654 Denys and his wife set up housekeeping at Pointe-aux-Pères, at a site that later became the golf course. He died there in 1688.

If you continue along the Acadian Coastal Route, also known as Route 134, you will come to ◆ **Daly Point Reserve,** just on the other side of Bathurst. This consists of 3¾ miles (6 km) of walking trails leading through more than one hundred acres (forty hectares) of saltmarsh, forest, and old farmland that is gradually reverting to its previous wild state. It is a great spot for nature lovers. Thousands of Canada geese stop by here in their fall migration, and the ringlet butterfly, found in only four salt-marshes in the world, can be seen here.

There are four trails and two paths, with the latter requiring more stable footwear. Scenery varies from a large gulch, which you cross by a footbridge, to twisting woodland paths, to the tamer boardwalks of the saltmarsh trails.

You won't get out of this region without hearing references to the phantom ship. (Recall that the tour boat in Dalhousie is called the *Phantom*.) For centuries people have claimed to see a ship on fire, far offshore. Skeptics argue that it is an optical illusion. The rest claim that it's the ghost of a ship lost long ago in battle.

THE HEART OF ACADIA

From the Daly Point Reserve, continue on Trunk 11 until you reach the outskirts of Caraquet. The drive should take about an hour; the road follows the coast quite closely until after Grande-Anse. When you reach a small community called Rivière du Nord, a sign on the right-hand side of the road will indicate the **◈ Acadian Historical Village.**

This is far more than just a historic re-creation of an Acadian village. Many of the forty buildings are actual restored Acadian homesteads from the 1800s, gathered into one village along with artifacts of bygone days, and some carefully constructed replicas. There are also a blacksmith shop dating from 1865, a school from 1869, and a reproduction of a Neguac cobbler's shop, circa 1875, where moccasins were the specialty.

The wonderful thing about this site is that all touch with the modern world has been kept at a remove, so that history is a living thing. Here the costumed guides re-create life as it was lived by Acadian settlers from 1780 to 1890. You'll see the home of a Scottish administrator whose powerful position in the community gave him the poshest accommodations.

A boat awaits repair in front of one dwelling, while the lady next door sweeps her steps with a broom made from whittling a young birch trunk. Elsewhere in the village you can watch as men split cedar to make roof shingles. Throughout the summer activities follow the pattern traditionally followed in an Acadian village: There are gatherings or working "bees" of various sorts, milling frolics intended to shrink large bolts of hand-loomed fabric, and agricultural fairs.

On the Acadian National Holiday, which falls on August 15, the staff re-creates a turning point in the history of the Acadian people: It is 1884. Actors debate the future of Acadie, include one playing a priest named Father Richard, the founder of Rogersville. Finally, after much debate, they agree on the priest's suggestion and choose a flag, an anthem, and a patron saint, strengthening their identity and creating a rallying point for cultural pride. Admission to the village is $8 for adults and $4.50 for children six to eighteeen years of age; children under six enter free; families pay $20.

Near the entrance to the Acadian Historical Village is a privately run wax museum, the ◈ **Musée de Cire d'Acadie.** This recently opened museum features eighty-six figurines in twenty-three different vignettes relating to the early life of the Acadians. The figurines were made by the same people who make wax models for Disney World. The developers of the museum have taken "lifelike" to its fullest extent. When you walk in front of a ship's cabins carrying settlers to Acadia, for example, it heaves just like a ship on the high seas. The museum is open daily from 9:00 A.M. to 7:00 P.M. Call (506) 727–6424 for more information.

Caraquet seems to be a mecca for Quebecois tourists in search of the picturesque. As such, you will find hints of the Quebec urban landscape that seem quite out of place here, including a club with exotic dancers, and Quebec-style restaurants.

Check out the **Crêpes Bretonne** restaurant, in nearby **Paquetville** (the birthplace of noted Acadian folksinger Edith Butler). This village is reached by turning onto Highway 325 directly after the Acadian Cultural Village, before Caraquet. The food served is typical of the Brittany-style crêpe places in Quebec City: meat or seafood and vegetables, served up in a cream sauce and then rolled in a thin French "pancake."

From Paquetville you can go on to Caraquet, where you probably are staying for the night. Or you can drive on to the junction with Highway 355, where you must turn left at the intersection and then right at Junction 217 to go in the direction of **Shippagan** via Highway 113.

There is an excellent natural harbor in Shippagan, which on the map looks almost like a collection of islands. In fact, the land is so low-lying that much of the area is covered in peat moss, so much so that they even have a peat moss festival, Le Festival de Tourbe, during which time they crown a peat moss queen and throw a big party. Peat moss is a big industry now, due to the growth of home gardening. You'll be able to tell when you're in peat moss territory, because the area seems unusually flat and boglike.

At the tail end of Shippagan you will come to a causeway that will bring you to **Ile Lamèque.** This is quite a picturesque island, popular with Quebecois because the region boasts several beaches with relatively warm water, due to their location in the shallow, narrow Baie des Chaleurs instead of right out on the gulf.

Once you get there stay on Highway 113 and drive along the northern side of the island. Soon you will see a small coastal village in which the church of ❖ **Ste.-Cécile** hosts an annual **International Festival of Baroque Music.** Despite its remote location, the festival features authentic period instruments and musicians from all over the world. Constructed in 1913, Ste.-Cécile's is noted not only for its wonderful accoustics but also for it's "naive" interior decor, executed in vibrant colors, the intensely painted handiwork of two artists. For details on the music festival, held in mid-July, call (506) 727–6622.

The village where you will find Ste.-Cécile's is called Petite Rivière de l'Ile. It ends just a short distance from the connection to **Ile Miscou.**

The ferry to Miscou no longer runs; it was recently replaced by a new bridge, which will make this summer paradise slightly more accessible. Still, its relative isolation lends it a bit of a Robinson Crusoe effect. The island is quite beautiful, as unspoiled as anyone could want. There are five beaches here.

The best one is located by taking the marked turnoff to ❖ **Miscou Island Camping,** just before the road turns abruptly right and leads to the lighthouse. The beach is accessed by a privately run campground. The parking fee of $2.50 entitles you to day use of the campgrounds' facilities. For overnight camping, with all hookups, the rate is $15. There are no lifeguards; take note that the big waves and strong current are quite hazardous. The water is warm and the beach is well worth the drive to the island.

Be sure to visit ❖ **Miscou Lighthouse,** the oldest still-functioning wooden lighthouse in the Maritimes. It overlooks a pristine natural setting, with miles of sandy shore. For a small fee you can climb to the top.

Once there, look out toward the flatland and to see the site of a Russian pilot's crash landing back in 1939. He was attempting to make the first solo transpolar flight from Moscow to New York when he ran into difficulty. He attempted to land on what appeared to be a good makeshift tarmac, but it turned out to be peat bog, unfrozen, and the plane was destroyed. He did however, officially make it across the polar ice cap, alive and without too much wear and tear on his body.

This is the most incredible place I have ever seen for beach-combing. The beach in front of the lighthouse is totally covered in driftwood of all sorts—so much so that you won't want to swim here. Try the beach at the campground to take a dip.

Slightly fewer than 900 people live on Ile Miscou. The French spoken on Miscou and Lamèque dates back to the era of the first Europeans in Canada, so you will have a chance to brush up on your Balzac.

Miscou's remote location has always been its biggest selling point. In the era of New France, it was favored as the ideal location for the illegal fur trade since it was so far away from Port Royal.

Its proximity to a rich fishing bank drew French fishermen here as far back as the early 1600s. Among the early entrepreneurs to invest time and effort in the island was Nicholas Denys, who had a post here before moving on to Cape Breton and then becoming governor.

Miscou, unfortunately, is only a summer paradise. In the winter it is blanketed by heavy snow, lashed by the bracing winds of the gulf. You'll notice that few trees attain much height.

After returning to Ile Lamèque, take Route 113 until you reach Exit 217. This is a fork in the road: Haut Pokemouche lies to the north. Turn left, heading south toward Pokemouche, and follow Highway 11 until you reach **Chatham,** or at least what used to be known as Chatham. (On newer maps Chatham, Newcastle, and Nelson-Miramichi have been rolled into one large community called Miramichi.)

In the midst of all this Acadian culture you will suddenly come upon an area of considerable Irish settlement, so much so that Chatham is the site of an **Irish Festival on the Miramichi.** Held in mid-July, this is the first and largest Irish festival in Canada. It features traditional music, culture, and entertainers from Ireland.

After Miramichi you have the option of taking Route 11 south as far as **Kouchibouguac National Park,** or driving along the coast on a pretty stretch of highway called Route 117. The reward of this latter course is an unsullied stretch of coast culminating in **Pointe-Sapin,** where you can snuggle up with nature. If you wish, you can camp or enjoy solitary stretches of beach here.

Pointe-Sapin is a charming Acadian village. The residents hold the Festival du Bon Pecheur (Festival of the Good Fisherman) each mid- to late July, purely as a local thing. The village is at the northern, coastal entrance to ✦ **Kouchibouguac National Park.** The protected dunes of the shoreline stretch like a long arm the length of the park. Along with watching rare bird life along the grassy dunes of Kouchibouguac, you can hike on any of ten trails, rent canoes, bikes, or paddleboats, or swim in lagoons holding the warmest salt water north of Virginia.

Much of the shoreline of this park is protected wilderness hosting a variety of rare flora and fauna, including the piping plover. There is an active beaver dam in the park, which always makes for fascinating viewing, and along the coast you can spot harbor and gray seals. For details call (506) 876–2443.

THE ACADIAN COAST

After enjoying the national park, continue south on Route 11 until you reach **Bouctouche,** the birthplace of two of New Brunswick's most famous natives: billionaire K. C. Irving and writer Antonine Maillet. Maillet's play *La Sagouine (The Cleaning Woman)*, won the highest acclaim possible in the French-speaking world, but its biggest impact by far is the fact that audiences have been unable to separate fact from fiction and are convinced that La Sagouine is a real person. So, on the nearby ✦ **Ile-aux-Puces,** reached by boardwalk and footbridge, you can enter an entire alternate universe devoted to her entitled **Le Pays de la Sagouine** or "The Land of the Cleaning Lady." Think of this as a 3-D play where you get to participate. By the time you've finished a meal of Acadian poutine râpées, pâtés à la viande, poutines à trou, and chicken fricot, and listened to some typical Acadian music and old-time storytelling, you will have a hard time distinguishing fact from fiction yourself. Prices are moderate.

Farther south along Route 11, in **Shediac,** the thing to do is visit ✦ **Cap Pelé Beach.** The water is consistently wonderful here, and the sand goes on forever. All summer long it's a good bet for a swim because it is situated along a very narrow and shallow stretch of the Northumberland Strait, giving it warm water.

Shediac has also laid claim to the title of "World's Lobster Capital," and while I've heard that before, only in Shediac will you have the opportunity to climb all over a gigantic lobster sculpture, situated along the village's main drag, overlooking a small inlet.

If you feel the need for an urban break, turn inland again on Route 15 west to **Moncton,** a surprisingly cosmopolitan and thoroughly pleasant little city, where the population is almost evenly divided between French- and English-speakers and bilingualism is a way of life. As a result, many nationwide services have gravitated to the area, adding to the dynamic feel of this cozy place.

Whether you are in Shediac or Moncton, you now must make a crucial decision: whether to explore the rest of New Brunswick's Fundy coast, to go on to Nova Scotia, or to head for Prince Edward Island. Here are the three alternative routes in brief:

1. If you are headed toward Nova Scotia, be sure to stop in Sackville for a visit to the ◆ **Sackville Waterfowl Park.** This is a fifty-acre (twenty-hectare) area of wetlands, which you explore on boardwalks, to which waterfowl and migratory birds fly in large numbers. Guides can explain the many intricacies of this ecosystem. The marshlands extend right up into the town. Mount Allison University is located here, with its well-recognized art college. Because of this the town is a good bet for souvenir shopping if you want some original art.

Just before the border with Nova Scotia you will come to ◆ **Fort Beausejour** in Aulac. You will find this on Trans-Canada Highway 2, in the heart of the windswept Tantramar Marshes. The fortress was the site of a major turning point in the history of New Brunswick: It was here that the British defeated the French and gained a toehold in the territory of New Brunswick. The fortifications here include earthworks, shaped like a five-sided star, and underground portions of the fortifications. The fort, which is a National Historic Site, has outdoor paintings depicting scenes from early battles. Admission is free.

2. To get to Prince Edward Island from Shediac, take Provincial Highway 15 until you connect to the TransCanada Highway 16, just a short distance from the link to P.E.I. The road is well marked.

3. If you are sticking to New Brunswick, then point your Pontiac south from Moncton along Route 114 until you reach ◆ **Hopewell Cape,** where the Petitcodiac River widens out to Shepedy Bay. This is the site of the "flowerpot rocks," which give a nature walk an added appeal. Actually chunks of land created by erosion resulting from the action of the Bay of Fundy's tides, these sandstone rocks tower above you at a height of four stories when the tide is out. At high tide, though, the site is unimpressive, and you'll wonder what all the fuss is about. This is the fate of sightseers along the Bay of Fundy—everything depends on the tides. The average difference between high and low tide is 36 feet (10.8 meters). When tides are low, you'll get a one-time chance to walk on the ocean floor.

Bear in mind that the tides here can take you by surprise. The change in water height can be sufficient to leave you stranded if you are not careful. Plan ahead by consulting a tide table (widely available in New Brunswick).

After Hopewell Cape you can return to Route 114 and drive to Riverside-Albert, where the highway joins Route 915 and continues on to Alma, where you can experience ◆ **Fundy National Park,** on the Bay of Fundy. There is an outdoor pool here filled with water pumped in from the bay and heated. While you swim you can catch some stunning views of the bay, but the area is otherwise quite isolated. Fundy National Park charges a fee of $6 per car per day or $18 for a four-day pass. Swimming is $2.75 per adult and $1.75 per child per day. Campers in the park swim free. From here you can continue through the park on another stretch of Provincial Highway 114 until you reach TransCanada Highway Route 2 a few miles outside Sussex.

If you happen to be here in Sussex and vicinity in the early fall, you will notice a large number of hot-air balloons in the air; balloonists hold a festival there annually. After Sussex you can return to Saint John via Route 1; now you will have done a complete circumnavigation of New Brunswick.

PRINCE EDWARD ISLAND

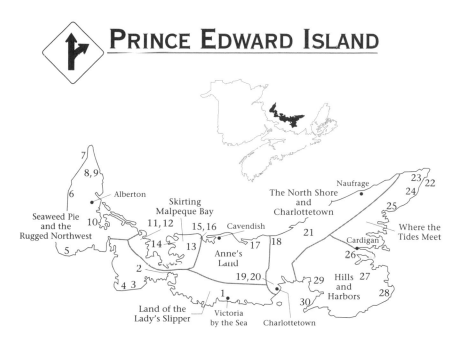

1. Victoria-by-the Sea
2. International Fox Museum and Hall of Fame
3. Cultural Pioneer Village
4. Cap-Egmont Bottle Houses
5. West Point Lighthouse
6. Irish Moss Interpretive Centre
7. Elephant Rock
8. Parish Church of St. Simon and St. Jude
9. Tignish Heritage Inn and Hostel
10. Mill River Golf Course
11. The Doctor's Inn Organic Market and Garden
12. Shoreline Sweaters & Tyne Valley Studio
13. Woodleigh
14. Malpeque Gardens
15. French Village
16. New London Seafood Restaurant
17. The Dunes Studio Gallery
18. Dalvay-by-the-Sea
19. Beaconsfield Historic House
20. Confederation Centre of the Arts
21. Bishop MacEachern National Historic Site
22. Arrowhead Lodge
23. Elmira Railway Museum
24. Basin Head Fisheries Museum
25. The Inn at Bay Fortune
26. Brudenell River Provincial Park
27. Buffaloland Provincial Park
28. Log Cabin Museum/Captain Garry's Seal and Bird Watching Cruises
29. Orwell Corner Historic Village
30. Point Prim Lighthouse/Lighthouse Artist Gallery and Chowder House

PRINCE EDWARD ISLAND

The descendants of the original settlers on Prince Edward Island (P.E.I) have clung so tenaciously to their traditional ways and manner of speech that you will find yourself imagining that you are in Ireland or Scotland or Brittany.

It isn't such a stretch of the imagination: Initial European settlements of French Acadians were followed by waves of Irish farmers and Scots. All of them have come to think of P.E.I. as the center of the universe—so much so that anywhere else is referred to, vaguely, as "away," and people from anyplace out of province are said to "come from away." And Prince Edward Island is simply referred to as "The Island." Even when those words are spoken aloud, you can tell they are in capital letters.

The key to getting off the beaten path in Prince Edward Island is to concentrate your travel at the two end points of The Island, thereby avoiding the outrageously popular tourist attractions clustered around the home of famous author Lucy Maud Montgomery and the sites related to her fictional heroine of *Anne of Green Gables*. First published in 1908, the book that made this red-haired orphan famous is in its ninety-ninth printing and has now been translated into dozens of languages. It holds cult status in Japan, where its place on the school curriculum and the spunky character of its heroine have guaranteed its supremacy in the hearts of young Japanese women. Thousands of Japanese make an annual pilgrimage to the Cavendish area of P.E.I. every summer.

Cavendish Beach is undoubtedly spectacular, but if you are looking for Anne, you may find her hard to spot among the legions of Japanese honeymooners, the bus-tour groups, the Ripley's Believe It or Not! Museum, and the many amusement parks. Since The Island has forty beaches to choose from, a good strategy is to aim for one of the less-frequented beaches. But if you are determined to visit Cavendish, try to get there before school closes at the end of June, or alternatively, go near the end of August. To ensure that you find lodging, book ahead through the Visitor Information Centre; call (800) 463–4PEI.

A little farther afield, however, and you are in the countryside that spawned the heart-warming series of Anne books that made The Island famous. Take particular note of the Scenic

Heritage Roads, which dot the various counties of P.E.I. These are characterized by the deep red clay (not so scenic in spring thaw or after several days of rain) and the pastoral countryside that has remained unchanged by the modern world. It is a constantly changing canvas: at times, all deep green and red clay; later in the summer, fields of purple and white potato flowers, ripening corn, and yellow hay.

If you fly over The Island, you'll be struck by the impression that you are looking at a diagonally pieced crazy quilt, boasting many shades of green and topstitched in the deep red of potter's clay. (To you, it may be mud, but to the potters who flock here, The Island's soil is heaven-sent inspiration. You'll find its hand-thrown products everywhere.)

If you visit The Island before June 1997, you will likely get there by car ferry from New Brunswick or Nova Scotia. After that date the "Fixed Link"—an 8-mile (13-km)–long bridge/causeway will replace the New Brunswick ferry, but it will take you to virtually the same spot on the island. Your point of arrival will therefore be either Borden or Wood Islands. From Borden it is only a short drive to the attractions in the western end of the province, while the east is quite accessible from Woods Islands.

Since the entire distance from one tip of P.E.I. to the other end of the crescent-shaped province is only 180 miles (288 km) and the landscape is either flat or gently rolling, it is the perfect place for a bicycle tour. This can last a few hours on a rented bike, or for the entire holiday on your own trusty steed.

Added to this are the many country bed-and-breakfast inn and farm vacations that make slow-paced travel particularly appealing. Most important (for cyclists of my caliber), you're never very far from a rest stop, a scenic view, or the next village. Half a dozen cycle-tour companies service people who visit The Island for this purpose.

When The Island railway was closed down recently, it was decided to convert the abandoned rail lines to combination bike paths and hiking trails, which will be used by skiers and snowmobilers in the winter. The many train stations left behind will now serve as rest areas for outdoor enthusiasts using the newly created trails.

The same thing that makes cycling so wonderful in Prince Edward Island makes giving road directions a hazardous business.

The Island consists of farmland from one end to the other, dotted with little communities, so the entire province is covered with a spider's web of roads. Since it is crescent-shaped, and as narrow across as 4 miles at one point, there are half a dozen ways to get anywhere—great for cyclists. If you don't like where you are, you can always take the next left and traverse the width of the entire province in less than twenty minutes.

We recommend either of two strategies for getting off the beaten path in Prince Edward Island. Either follow the route we have mapped out in a clockwise direction from Borden, with Borden at six o'clock on the dial; or follow the same routing in reverse from the Wood Islands ferry landing, on the eastern end of the province. If there is something you want to bypass, simply detour onto one of the many rural routes that crisscross the province.

LAND OF THE LADY'S SLIPPER

If you travel to **Borden** from New Brunswick, you will either have the opportunity to be one of the first to travel on the world's longest continuous multispan bridge, or a good chance to examine it undergoing the final stage of construction as your ferry sails just to the right of it. Once in Borden, if you so much as blink, you risk missing a charming little fishing village just fifteen minutes from the ferry landing. Therefore, even though I've mapped out a tour of The Island's western end first, I am going to suggest that you make one small detour east as soon as you get off the boat in Borden.

Simply because of its out-of-the-way location, between the two ferries, few explore the many and varied charms of the tiny unspoiled fishing village of ◆ **Victoria-by-the-Sea.** Established along a British colonial-style grid pattern, it is quite compact, which makes for pleasant strolling. Just park your car and drift around.

What Victoria-by-the-Sea has to offer is four square blocks of quaint little nooks and crannies, a tearoom, cafes, and a theater, (**The Victoria Playhouse** presents popular theater nightly all summer long). The **Studio Gallery,** on a lane to your right as you walk up from the shore, displays the work of a number of local artists, etchings, oils, and acrylics—some representational, some surrealistic. There are also pottery, antiques, craft and quilt shops, and other appealing stores. You can't miss anything by simply wandering around this tiny village. The wharf has now been spruced up to house a restaurant, but the winds have so far kept the outdoor deck from being a favored dining spot.

The little harbor's range light houses the **Victoria Seaport Museum,** where you can chat with the students who run the museum and catch up on the local scene. This is the second-oldest lighthouse on P.E.I., and photographs of some of its most reliable keepers are displayed here—one man put in fifty years on the job. The lighthouse exhibits navigational aids from the 1920s, including a kerosene lamp used in the range light for many years. You can climb to the top to see the modern light or just check out the harbor from the second floor. Admission is free, though donations are welcome.

The village boasts several beaches as well as a lobster pound, meaning a good supply of fresh lobster at the local eating establishments. You can also watch chocolates being made at **Island Chocolates.** The shop also sells a variety of locally-produced herbal vinegars and specialty jams. They are open from 10:00 A.M. to 8:00 P.M. Phone at (902) 658–2320.

The village's foremost accommodations are in an inn dating back to 1900. The **Orient Hotel** is one of the last two original hotels operating in P.E.I. (The establishment is now part of a network of Heritage inns in Atlantic Canada.) There are six guest rooms, all with private bath, a dining room, and a tearoom serving that ubiquitous Island beverage as well as freshly baked desserts. **Mrs. Profitt's Tea Room** is named for the daughter of the hotel's founders. Mrs. Profitt ran the hotel from 1926 to 1953. Teas from Mrs. Profitt's are sufficiently popular that its blends are now being produced and marketed. The hotel operates on the modified American plan, with scrumptious, full country breakfasts. Cycle-touring note: There is storage for bicycles. Reserve a room by calling (800) 565–ORIENT.

For more details write to Orient Hotel, Box 162, Charlottetown, P.E.I. C1A 7K4.

Innkeepers Lee Jolliffe and Darrell Tschirhart have a wealth of information on the village's events and sights. Lee has a Ph.D. in Museum Studies and consults with tourism operators all over The Island. "The special thing about this village is that it is an unspoiled seaport," says Lee. "Its four square blocks and harbor have not changed much in the last century." Homes are sold only to year-round residents, and there is a restriction on further growth, ensuring that this rare gem of a village remains just that.

After enjoying Victoria turn west and backtrack the fifteen minutes toward Borden and the western end of The Island.

If you want to skip Victoria-by-the-Sea or leave it to the end of your stay on The Island, then turn west immediately after leaving the ferry in Borden. Turning west will take you briefly to **Summerside** and from then to the small fishing villages and cozy beaches of the western end of the island.

In the nineteenth century the economic mainstay of Summerside was its shipbuilding industry. You can relive some of that era at **Spinnakers' Landing,** which offers an opportunity to explore an interpretive center showing the shipbuilding techniques of the early 1800s. While the development is recent rather than historic, the harborside shops stock a variety of crafts and gift items. Harbor cruises can be booked on the spot. In front of the shops is a play area comprised of a jungle-gym in the shape of a boat. On the morning I visited, flocks of children were playing tug-of-war while their parents explored the shops.

Although Summerside is a decidedly small town, its streets are graced with stately old homes that recall a time of wealth and ease. These date back not only to the years when it was the center of The Island's shipbuilding trade but also to when it was the focus of the lucrative silver fox industry. That era is depicted in charcoal drawings, photographs, and folk art at the ❖ **International Fox Museum and Hall of Fame,** 286 Fitzroy Street, 3 blocks back from the harbor.

The industry's boom started in the late 1800s and reached its peak in the 1920s. Breeding pairs of the top-quality foxes were even traded for houses; one pair fetched an outstanding $35,000 in the open market. At its height the industry constituted one-sixth of The Island's economic base, bringing wealth to many Summerside furriers.

The Island was the site of the first successful fur farm in the world, beginning in the 1870s with the capture of a pair of wild black foxes. A little over a decade later, experimentation finally resulted in a successful breeding program. The results of these early studies form the basis of all current fur-farming methods in the world today. The industry continues to this day with just over sixty fur farmers on the island. For details about the museum, call (902) 436–2400. The suggested admission is $1.00.

Fifteen minutes' drive west on Route 11 from Summerside will take you to **Mont Carmel,** site of the ❖ **Cultural Pioneer Village.** The village is 1 mile (1.5 km) past Our Lady of Mont Carmel Church. The route is marked by a logo depicting the lady's slipper, a typical island flower, for which Lady Slipper Drive (Route 11) is named. If you chance upon one of these flowers, don't pick it—it would take thirteen years for a new flower to grow in its place!

The first European settlers on The Island were Acadians, settlers from France's Atlantic coast. While many were exiled shortly after the British won possession of The Island, a number escaped into the woods with the help of native peoples and then quietly reestablished normal lives. The Acadian presence is still significant, with 17 percent of Island residents descendants from these first European settlers.

The re-created village is located on the actual site of a village founded in 1812 by Acadians who moved here from nearby St.-Eleanors. The rustic structures of "Le Village," as it is known locally, reproduce the Acadian settlement from that early era. They include a blacksmith shop, a store, and a school, all built of logs. Be sure to step into the little Acadian church, with its altar made entirely of logs; it is striking in design and strangely reminiscent of a pipe organ.

In the center of the complex is an open air "theater," where massive murals depicting scenes from the early life of the Acadians are displayed. Among them is the story of Evangeline, the now-famous Acadian heroine who was separated from her husband on her wedding day. The real Evangeline became a nun in Philadelphia and was reunited with her husband on his deathbed, many years later. The village is open daily from 9:30 A.M. to 7:00 P.M. from mid-June to mid-September. Admission is $3.00 for adults, half price for children ages 6 and older; children under 6 enter for free. Call (800) 567–3228.

The restaurant **Étoile de Mer** serves traditional Acadian fare. These include such hits as *rapure,* a potato pie popular throughout Acadian regions, and Quebecois specialties like *poutin.* During the summer it offers a dinner theater. Call (902) 854–2227 for hours and reservations.

47

Just 3 miles (5 km) farther west down Route 11 (Lady Slipper Drive) from Mont Carmel, you will come to Cap-Egmont, home of the ✦ **Cap-Egmont Bottle Houses,** the masterpiece of a stellar attempt at recycling.

You mustn't pass up the chance to consider at length the single-mindedness of someone who collects and then cements together 25,000 glass bottles to form buildings. Originally the work of the late Edouard T. Arsenault, a retired fisherman, the structures include a spectacular little chapel complete with altar and pews, a six-gabled house, and a spacious tavern.

The original inspiration for the project came from a bottle house on Vancouver Island, but that climate was far more benign in the winter months. Much of the original complex has needed restoring due to the impact of The Island's severe winters on the unique building materials. Two of the three structures have undergone major repair.

Hobbyists in particular will love this place, if for no other reason than to reassure themselves that they have yet to get truly carried away with their obsession. The three bottle houses and the gardens, which at their peak feature more than fifty varieties of flowers, are open daily from 10:00 A.M. to 6:00 P.M. (There are slightly longer hours in June; call for details.) A small admission is charged. In the off-season phone (902) 854–2254, in summer (902) 854–2987.

SEAWEED PIE AND THE RUGGED NORTHWEST

Continuing along this sparsely populated stretch of shoreline will take you to the black and white ✦ **West Point Lighthouse,** located in the **Cedar Dunes Provincial Park.** This is the only functioning lighthouse in Canada that also serves as an inn. Built in 1875 and operated by the Coast Guard, this is one of The Island's tallest lighthouses, measuring 69 feet. It now includes a museum and gift shop. The museum holds maps, tools, logbooks, and a collection of other artifacts that recount the story of The Island's lighthouses and the era of sail. Here you can read about the fascinating characters who ran the light, among them "Lighthouse Willie," the great-grandfather of Carol Livingstone, who spearheaded the move to turn the lighthouse into an inn.

Lighthouse Willie held the job of lighthouse keeper from 1875 to 1925, never missing one night of work in fifty years. He was

Cap-Egmont Bottle House

the father of eight children and ran a farm 1.5 miles (2 km) away. During the summer the family came to stay at the lighthouse, and his wife brought a beautiful organ there for entertainment. After passing through many family hands, that organ has been restored to its original lighthouse location.

Admission is $2.00 for adults, but if you eat lunch in the restaurant downstairs, your visit to the lighthouse is free.

There are nine rooms where overnight guests can stay. All guest rooms have private baths, and two have whirlpool baths. The rooms have been decorated to re-create the era of the lightkeepers, with old-fashioned touches and handmade quilts. Considering the incomparable view and the opportunity to fall asleep to the hypnotic lapping of the waves, you really ought to phone ahead for reservations; call (902) 859–3605. Rates are moderate. Write for more information to The West Point Lighthouse, O'LEARY, RR2, P.E.I. C0B 1V0. The lighthouse is located on Route 14.

This site offers even more. The beach at Cedar Dunes Provincial Park is quite lovely and well enough off the beaten path to offer a quiet respite from civilization. The park is protected by legislation because of its environmental significance. The **Cedar Bog** contains a fragile ecosystem that you can explore through guided nature trails and the interpretive program.

While visiting the park and lighthouse, you can also satisfy your urge for souvenir collecting at the **West Point Lighthouse Craft Guild,** located to the right of the lighthouse. The shop features work by several local artisans. To confirm hours of operation, call locally (902) 859–3742.

The end of the province has wonderfully pristine fishing villages and presents a wealth of photographic opportunities. The coastal villages, which are particularly appealing, are clustered along the western coast, where Irish moss is a big source of income. Fishermen harvest this seaweed, which is then processed for its carrageenin, a substance used in the making of ice cream and other food products. Depending on which way the wind is blowing, you will see the moss being harvested either by boats that skirt the shoreline, by men raking it by hand, or by men using horses to gather it up. The gathering of Irish moss is a surprisingly lucrative career. One man waiting to unload his truck at the "plant" mentioned that his truckload took four days to gather and was worth $1,800.

On **Miminegash,** on Route 152, you can learn all about the industry in the ❿**Irish Moss Interpretive Centre,** which is fronted by **The Seaweed Pie Café.** The interpretive center is open from 10:00 A.M. until 7:00 P.M. Monday to Friday. Stop by and have seaweed pie. I'm serious. Eating seaweed pie is like getting your ears pierced: Regardless of how you feel about it at the moment, you'll be happy with the results. More accurately called "Irish moss pie," it is something like a custard or cream pie with a graham-cracker crust and a fruit topping. Since the custard is made from the same substance that is used in the manufacture of ice cream, it's really not bad at all. Take note unlike the interpretive centre, the Seaweed Pie Café does not open until noon (Monday to Friday). They close at 7:00 P.M.

The image of the island is one of pastoral splendor and potato fields, so the terrain at the far western tip of the province is far more rugged than most people expect.

If you travel to a small coastal village called **Norway,** along Route 14, you will see the ❖ **Elephant Rock,** carved from the deep red cliffs of The Island's western coast. (The red color comes from the high iron content of the soil.) Take note that the Elephant Rock is not to be found at the location currently indicated on The Island's tourist map. Rather, it is farther north, on a secondary road one left turn after Seacow Pond.

The Rock looks truly like an elephant, right down to the hairy back (thanks to the grass growing on the top of the mound). A dirt road leads down to the shore, where you can walk around the Rock and get a good look at it. Note the underside. To make sure that the sea won't destroy this new attraction, locals have reinforced the underside of the Rock to protect it against the action of the tides.

Now continue north to the rock reef of The Island's northern tip and the historic **North Point Lighthouse** at North Cape. A wide rock reef extends along the shoreline for 1 mile (1.6 km) offshore; on warm days people will wade around in the shallow water as far back as they can get, trying to take pictures.

You will not be able to enter this still-functioning lighthouse, but the view is still worth dropping by for. And just as you drive up to the lighthouse, you may notice the whirligigs to your left. This is the location of the **Atlantic Wind Test Site.** The twirling structures dotting the heath are gigantic wind turbines that are being tested and evaluated for use in harvesting the wind's energy.

The interpretive center at the North Point Lighthouse includes a video explaining the work of the wind-power laboratory, and guides will answer questions, but the actual lab is closed to the public. The entry fee to the center is $2.00, which includes admittance to an aquarium where you can see local aquatic species like lobsters and mussels. Upstairs, the **Wind and Reef** restaurant is reputed to be good but expensive. The Wind and Reef's phone number is (902) 882–3535. They are open from May 28 to October 10. Hours vary. Sunday to Friday, they open from 11:30 A.M. to 10:00 P.M. On Saturday they stay open until midnight.

From here turn south again, but this time take the left fork onto Route 12, where you will come to some utterly unspoiled fishing villages, including Kildare Capes, Jude's Point, Tignish, and Anglo Tignish, as well as the wonderfully uncrowded beaches of Fisherman's Haven and Jacques Cartier Provincial Park. Fisherman's Haven, between Tignish Shore and Kildare Capes, has picnicking facilities.

There are a fine beach and accommodations at the **Jacques Cartier Provincial Park.** On a blazing hot day in August, you'll see perhaps a dozen people at this lovely spot. The water is quite warm here, and the atmosphere is low-key.

While in **Tignish** visit the ◆ **Parish Church of St. Simon and St. Jude,** which has a large pipe organ dating back to 1882. Its pipes are up to 16 feet (5 m) tall. The church is a large brick building located at the corner of Maple and Church streets, near the intersection with the highway.

Its chief historical significance lies in the fact that the organ is a product of the first French Canadian school of organ construction. It is the largest of four tracker-action organs built by the famous Louis Mitchell of Montreal. These pipe organs with huge bellows were operated by a team of two men who pumped air during the performance. Control of the organ was achieved with foot pedals. Many of these organs were either altered to electro-pneumatic instruments or destroyed as modernity and technology cut a swathe through tradition. This is the only one of its kind outside Quebec that is still intact. Only after most of these large pipe organs were gone from the face of the earth did musicologists begin yearning for a return to a purer form of organ music, recalling the era of Bach.

The sound of the pipes is greatly enhanced by the neo-Gothic vaults of the church. Legends abound about the arrival of the organ in such an out-of-the-way community. One such story holds that it arrived by accident and it was only when it was uncrated on the church lawn that a decision was made to keep it. Its assembly cost $2,400 at the time. Today it is considered priceless because of its historical significance, but its projected replacement cost is estimated to be roughly $100,000.

You can indulge your passion for sublime music if you happen to be in the neighborhood on a Sunday. There are occasional concerts at other times as well. Since the church is not always occupied, you can check concert time at this number (the parish house), (902) 882–2049.

Just behind this church is a bed and breakfast that was once a convent. It is now called the ◆ **Tignish Heritage Inn and Hostel.** There is lots of space for travelers, including an actual dormitory on the third floor that a group of twenty could use. Groups of people traveling together by bicycle, for example, would find this a convenient rest stop. Although this one-time nun's cloister was built in 1868, it has been considerably revamped, such that thirteen rooms have their own private bath and shower.

The convent was built so that nuns from Montreal could come and teach in the area. It became a residence for the nuns and was the site of instruction until 1966. It was then used purely as a residence for the sisters until it closed its doors in 1991. When it was taken over in 1993 by a nonprofit group called Tignish Initiatives, careful attention was paid to the preservation of the original structure, such that organizers received a 1994 Architectural Preservation Award from the board of governors of the Prince Edward Island Museum and Heritage Foundation. Rates are standard, with a continental breakfast included. For more information or to reserve a spot, call (902) 882–2491 or write to Nicole Gaudet, P.O. Box 398, Tignish, P.E.I. C0B 2B0.

Just south of Jacques Cartier Provincial Park is **Alberton,** the one-time western terminus of The Island's now defunct railway, which is gradually being turned into the **Confederation Trail.** From here you can take a deep-sea fishing trip for a reasonable fee ($18 per adult, $15 for seniors, and $12 for kids). There are numerous boats on The Island for hire. In Alberton try *The Andrew's Mist,* which is government-inspected. It is operated by Captain Craig Avery. Equipment is supplied free; you get to keep your cleaned, filleted, and bagged catch. For more information call (902) 853–2307.

In Alberton you can also watch skilled craftspeople making maple products from candleholders to plates and clocks. The **Leavitts' Maple Tree Craft** facility is 4,000 square feet in size, full of craft items and works-in-progress. Getting to know Herb Leavitt is half the fun.

If you are planning to stay in Alberton, consider lodging at a farm-turned-bed-and-breakfast. The **Cold Comfort Farm** is a minute's drive away from Route 12, on Matthews Road. Overlooking potato fields and the small river that flows into the village, the house was built during the silver fox boom.

The owners, Kennedy and Marilyn Wells, are former foreign correspondents who decided to return to the good life on Prince Edward Island. Early in this decade the barn burned down and the underinsured livestock were lost, so the Welles started taking in guests. The home is charmingly decorated and packed with interesting books. The name of the farm is borrowed from the title of a book by Briton Stella Gibbons, a 1930s cult-classic satire of the melodramatic pastoral romances of the time. (Several copies of the much-loved parody are in evidence around the house for your perusal.) Rooms prices are standard, with large country breakfasts included. For reservations call (902) 853–2803.

Apart from potatoes and fictional heroines, the rolling green farmland and deep red soil of Prince Edward Island have also given birth to a number of excellent golf courses. These are affordable, accessible, and a big hit with visitors and residents alike. Even at their most expensive, the courses never exceed $40 in greens fees for an entire day.

A number of championships have been held on courses on The Island. Of these, *Golf Digest* has deemed the ◆ **Mill River Golf Course** to be "Atlantic Canada's most challenging." It was the site of the 1994 Canadian Women's Championship. You can reach it from Alberton by turning south on Route 12 and exiting to Highway 136 South.

Bounded by beautiful stands of hardwood and spruce, this course features a series of spring-fed ponds down the eighth fairway. Golfers who goof and get their ball in the water are invited to take a drink of the spring water. The greens fees are $25 to $30, including tax. You can book ahead at (800) 377–8339.

Mill River Golf Course is near a Scenic Heritage drive. When you exit the golf course onto Highway 136 east, travel to Fortune Cove. Here you can take the clay Heritage road by turning right and driving southeast until you reach Highway 142. At this junction, turn left and drive east.

So-called Scenic Heritage Drives dot the province and are a good opportunity to experience the old Prince Edward Island. The clay roads are generally covered with a canopy of trees casting shade across the unspoiled beauty of farmlands that ramble down to the water. You'll have views of old farmhouses and barns, paint fading and cracking off, and herds of grazing dairy cows. Some fields are carefully laid out in row after row of potato plants. It's like time travel. This is the land that Lucy Maud Montgomery wrote about so lovingly.

These roads are best traveled after a brief spell of rain, when they're not too wet to turn into mud yet not so dry as to be a dust bowl.

This particular Heritage road is known as the "John Joe Road" or the "Hackney Road." It is bordered by fields of grain and potatoes, alternated with woodland to create a habitat much beloved by the grey partridge and the ruffed grouse.

After about 1.5 miles (2.2 km) on this little road, you will join Kelly Road, also known as Route 142. Before 1912 this was a cart track that lead to a homestead in the woods. Near its southern end you will find traces of an old stagecoach route.

SKIRTING MALPEQUE BAY

At the time of the European settlement of Prince Edward Island, the Micmac of the area were nomadic, hunting game and fishing over a wide range. They settled for only short periods of time in any one area, as the seasons dictated. The white settlers, on the other hand, set about clearing the land and divided it up into lots for farming, establishing a system of ownership completely foreign to the Micmac. As more land was cleared and fences built, the population of wild animals diminished. The Micmac way of life was imperiled.

Finally, Sir James Montgomery, a wealthy British landlord, gave them the use of **Lennox Island,** rent free. By 1800 a missionary had persuaded some of them to live year-round on the island. Seventy years later, after much petitioning of the government and several attempts to resolve the land issue, Lennox Island was purchased for the Micmacs. It lies just north of Route 12.

If you continue driving east along Route 12, you will see an exit to a secondary road, Route 167. Take this exit and you will soon reach a beautiful, pastoral little village called **Tyne Valley,** population 200.

Here you will find ❧ **The Doctor's Inn Organic Market and Garden,** operated by Paul and Jean Offer. The "Inn" part of the place is a bed-and-breakfast establishment, making use of the charming former home of the village doctor, built in 1860.

For the environmentally conscious, the Offers provide a number of activities, from gardening to gourmet meals. One of their most popular features is a five-hour workshop on the cultivation and use of organic herbs, the intricacies of organic gardening, composting, and safe, effective insect control. This is part of a two-night stay, with two suppers included.

55

Nonguests may dine by reservation, with meals a mix of health-conscious international and classical cuisine. Although the menu choices are limited, the restaurant has been recommended in a number of national publications. Paul and Jean Offer say, "The gardens provide most of the items for our dinners and also guarantee the freshness we have become noted for." Prices are moderate, and they are open year-round. It's a small place, so try to book ahead. Phone (902) 831–3057.

If you aren't up to a five-hour workshop, opt for a free, informal tour of the three-acre market garden. Organized tours are set for 1:00 P.M. Sunday and Wednesday, from late June to September. If you roam around in the garden, take note of the red "balls" on the fruit trees, these are highly effective insect traps that eliminate the need for bug spray.

While in this charming little hamlet, be sure to check out ◆**Shoreline Sweaters & Tyne Valley Studio,** just a minute's drive farther down Route 12. This is the birthplace of Prince Edward Island's answer to the Fair Isle sweater: the copyrighted motif features stylized lobsters, on pure Island-spun handcrafted woolen.

You can see the famous lobster sweaters popping up in many of the Island's Visitor Information Centres. The results are charming and subtle. Designer Lesley Dubey has often had to point out the lobsters in the complex motif, variations of which are found in cardigans, round-neck pullovers, and shawl-collar pullovers. "Once people realize it's really a little lobster, they really like it, more than if it was a big lobster sprawled across their back or chest."

The cardigans are graced with pewter buttons, themselves decorated with little lobsters. New creations include sweaters with lady's-slipper and lupin designs.

The shop also sells other craft items, including weaving, baskets, and their own wildflower honey. "We keep bees, and have customers who spend summers here, then come and get a supply to take home." The nectars are gathered by "over-wintered" bees, which make their honey from the profusion of wildflowers that make Tyne Valley particularly idyllic. Call (902) 831–2950.

Leaving Tyne Valley via Route 12, you will be skirting **Malpeque Bay,** with its many fishing communities. If you continue along the Blue Heron Drive, you will soon find yourself at the far eastern end of the bay, at a fork in the road and the village of Kensington.

From here you have the option of visiting gardens or large-scale models of castles, or backtracking and visiting both. There are also a fine beach and campground at the mouth of Malpeque Bay.

If you take Route 101 to Burlington and then turn right onto Route 234, you will come to ◆ **Woodleigh.** Large-scale replicas provide hours of fun in the middle of the countryside. Walk amid "York Minster Cathedral," Scotland's "Dunvegan Castle" and the "Tower of London" and never get out of breath. These replicas reach the height of an NBA basketball star and cover a 33-acre (13-hectare) country garden setting. Some of the little castles have interesting replicas inside. The Tower of London portion, for example, which comprises several of the towers where the famous and infamous were kept in dungeons, also houses a set of "crown jewels." The chopping block where several of Henry VIII's wives lost their heads is reproduced outside.

Colonel Ernest Johnstone, the gentleman who built these replicas as a retirement project, passed away in his eighties, just five years after he completed the "Temple of Flora," which opens on the gardens. Admission is about $7.00 for adults and $4.00 for children over 6 (younger children are admitted free). Call (902) 836–3401.

Plan ahead to arrive on a Sunday if you would like to enjoy an outdoor concert at the site. The **Woodleigh Concerts on the Green** series start at 2:00 P.M., during the summer months. The small cost can be added to the admission price of a visit to the replicas. The entertainment includes Acadian folkloric and traditional Celtic music, both of which are dynamic forces on The Island.

Just in front of Woodleigh, you will see a marking for a Scenic Heritage Road. This is the Millman Road, which is a handy shortcut to Route 20, also known as the Blue Heron Drive.

If it's gardens you want, take Route 20 west until you reach Malpeque. Here you will find the lovely ◆ **Malpeque Gardens.** The three acres (1¼ hectares) of meticulously tended gardens are level enough that they are wheelchair accessible. This is also a good rest stop for those traveling with children, because the gardens also feature swings, a slide, and a children's garden, which has a "Pumpkin Carriage" and statues of Snow White and her short friends.

Annuals, perennials, dahlias, rose gardens, and some prizewinning begonias are part of the attraction. (The dahlias are massive items and quite impressive.) You'll sense that you are getting close to the traditional stomping ground of author Lucy Maud Montgomery, because a miniature green-gabled house punctuates the "Anne of Green Gables Gardens," which features floral beds common to the author's era.

Farther along Blue Heron Drive, you'll come to Malpeque itself and then to **Cabot Beach Provincial Park.** This has small beaches and is far enough off the tourist trail that it is a pleasantly quiet spot for camping. Its **Twin Shores/Cabot Beach Provincial Park** is really two quiet campsites, far from the madding crowd that congregates during the tourist high season at Cavendish. These red-sand beaches are opposite each other across a sheltered bay and offer warm water and an unhurried rest only a few miles north of Summerside. The beaches—indeed, the entire shoreline—has a shelf of hard clay upon which bathers can walk from beach to beach, pausing along the way at sheltered spots where the water is bathtub-warm.

Because they are both small campsites, it is advisable to book in advance, especially during the high season. The numbers to call are (902) 836–4142 for Twin Shores, (902) 836–5635 for Cabot Beach.

ANNE'S LAND

Past Darnley Basin and headed east you will soon come to Park Corner, still on Route 20. Several sites in this village recall The Island's famous author, but in a sedate way as compared to the mecca near Lucy Maud Montgomery's fabled home in Cavendish. They are less hectic alternatives if you happen to be an "Anne Fan."

The first one that you will come to is the **Anne of Green Gables Museum at Silver Bush.** Silver Bush (so named by Montgomery) was the home of the writer's aunt and was built in 1872. The place remains much as it was in Montgomery's time. Because the author was married in the parlor, young Japanese couples often arrange with the owner to tie the knot there, but otherwise the house is not a slick, professionally assembled museum but, rather, a cozy old home. There is a little tearoom for visitors as well as wagon rides on site. When you peek at the lovely old bedsteads and furnishings, it isn't hard to understand why Montgomery said her ideal home would be an exact duplicate of this.

The farmhouse overlooks the pond for which she coined the name "The Lake of Shining Waters." After you leave this

58

museum, the little pond will be on your left. Just after passing over a little stream, you will come to the next "Anne site."

The **Lucy Maud Montgomery Heritage Museum** was the home of Montgomery's grandfather, an Island senator. Still owned by the family, it has been turned into an "attraction." There is far less to see here relative to the famous author, but it's still quite a substantial old place. It holds many family heirlooms and is largely unchanged since the time of the author's frequent visits, which she wrote about in her journals.

Both homes charge a small admission fee. Call (902) 886–2807 or (902) 886–2752 for more information.

Just after Park Corner and continuing along Route 20, you will come to ◆ **French Village,** a picturesque fishing community overlooking New London Bay. Apart from the photographic possibilities, you are directly across the water from the national park, which comprises several seemingly endless beaches, and the majority of the sites relating to *Anne of Green Gables.*

A small village called **Stanley Bridge** is a good place to stay if you want to visit the Cavendish area. Located at the junction of Routes 6, 224, and 254, the village is a mere 5 miles (8 km) west of Cavendish. Here you will find the cottages of **Stanley Bay Country Resort.**

All of the cottages as well as a completely renovated motel have been constructed from lumber cut from the owners' own woodlot, with rustic pine walls and floors and cathedral ceilings in an open-beam country style. With such amenities as hot tubs and two playgrounds for children, owners warn visitors to book as far ahead as January for week-long stays. Rates are moderate. Write Rick and Tina Roberts, Kensington, RR #6 P.E.I. C0B 1M0; call or fax (800) 361–2882.

In the resort complex you will find two craft studios, **Stanley Bridge Studios** and **Blue Heron Pottery.** The studios upstairs are a good bet for locally made quilts as well as reproduction tin lighting, pewter, hand-forged iron, and other collectibles to create a country-style decor in a house. The downstairs holds the studio of potter Darren Matheson, where visitors can watch Island clay being thrown. The potters here favor deep, sensuous colours like midnight black, vivid blues, and pastel pinks and greens for their earthenware. The studio offers pottery demonstrations. For details or to confirm hours of operation, call (902) 886–2800.

Other craft shops in the area include **Granny's Trunk** on Route 6, west of Cavendish. This store, which features some prize-winning quilts, also sells home-baked goodies. It's located 1¼ miles (2 km) from the intersection at Stanley Bridge, in the direction of Cavendish. The phone number is (902) 886–2030. Open 8:00 A.M. to 5:00 P.M.

The **Spinning Wheel Craft Shop** is housed in the **Village Vista Building** right at the highway intersection in Stanley Bridge. It offers not only the usual fare of crafts but also a selection of Maritimes music and books. Phone (902) 886–2159. Open 10:00 A.M. to 5:00 P.M.

On this end of The Island, the eatery with the reputation for the freshest fish is the ♦ **New London Seafood Restaurant.** Situated right on the wharf in New London, it gives new meaning to the phrase "catch of the day." It's a huge place, with a seating capacity of one hundred. Two full walls of windows yield a spectacular view of the bay, featuring the comings and goings of the local fishing fleet and pleasure boats. Owners Lawrence and Roger Cole, two brothers, run this family-style restaurant.

Lawrence points out that this area is noted for its Island Blue cultured mussels as well as Malpeque oysters, which are exported worldwide. The chowders in this end of the country are delicious and reasonably priced at roughly $3.00 for a small bowl and $5.50 for a large bowl. The restaurant also has a traditional lobster supper for roughly $20.00, with the option of a second lobster for around $7.00 more. These dinners include potato salad, either seafood chowder or mussels, rolls, and homemade pie. Lobsters also find their way into sandwiches and salad rolls. The restaurant is open from mid-June until the end of September. To reserve, phone (902) 886–3000.

Two antiques shops are also in the neighbourhood. On Route 238, off Route 6, you will find **Linden Cove Antiques.** It specializes in high-quality mahogany, walnut, and oak furniture, and tableware.

Returning to Route 6, in the direction of New London, you'll soon come to **New London Crafts and Antiques.** Here are folk art, collectibles, quilts, and, for the travel-weary, a tearoom for a nice spot of tea and a nibble, before looking over the memorabilia, not to mention Anne dolls. Open from 9:00 A.M. until 8:00 P.M. during the summer months.

If dolls aren't your style but you are interested in looking at or buying a painting, the best selection is at ❦ **The Dunes Studio Gallery,** overlooking Brackley Beach on Route 15. You cannot miss this building: Virtually all windows, it is a contemporary masterpiece complete with spiral staircase, an excellent view, and a substantial water garden outside.

The works of many prominent provincial artists are on display here. Their works include The Island's most high-end paintings, pottery, crafts, sculptures, photography, and prints. The Dunes has a cafe, a roof garden, and a fourth-floor lookout. It opens for the summer in May, closes for the winter in October, and will open at other times of the year by appointment. From June to September, the Dunes is open from 9:00 A.M. to 10:00 P.M. In May and October, it is open from 10:00 A.M. to 6:00 P.M. Phone (902) 672–2586.

THE NORTH SHORE AND CHARLOTTETOWN

To bypass the most heavily visited end of the national park but still sample The Island's best beaches, continue east along the coastal route until you reach ❦ **Dalvay-by-the-Sea.** This is a small, intimate, and charming establishment at the far eastern end of the park, a short drive from the gateway. Dalvay overlooks Tracadie Bay and is reached by a left turn after Grand Tracadie.

At the turn of the century people from other parts of the country discovered Prince Edward Island's unique charms and the opportunity it offered to get away from it all. Some wealthy families built large summer homes here. Dalvay-by-the-Sea is the most notable of these, built in 1895. It was originally the home of the American president of Standard Oil, born in Scotland, who found in Dalvay the perfect home away from home. He therefore named it for his own birthplace. The home eventually changed hands several times and became a hotel.

Along with the calm atmosphere and lovely vista, Dalvay boasts an excellent restaurant, thanks to renowned Australian chef Richard Kemp. There are canoes and croquet sets, big old-fashioned bathtubs, and the massive stone hearths of half a dozen fireplaces.

Fans of the television show *The Road to Avonlea* will recognize the Dalvay, where it is depicted as the "White Sands Hotel." This Victorian hotel is the Island's only seaside inn and unquestionably one of the most elegant country inns in all the east coast of

61

Canada. Reserve rooms by writing to D. Thompson, Box 8, Little York, P.E.I. C0A 1P0; or call (902) 672–3315. Rates are deluxe.

From Dalvay you have the choice of cutting across the province to Charlottetown or continuing east to the more remote fishing villages and beaches of the far eastern end of The Island. Traveling from Dalvay to Charlottetown is a simple matter. Get onto Route 6 and drive in the direction of Bedford. Just after Bedford turn right onto Route 2 and continue on into Charlottetown.

Charlottetown may be the provincial capital, but it is a far cry from a big city. Its streets were so narrow in the early part of this century that when cars came on the scene, they were banned from the entire province in 1913. This law was not repealed until 1919.

It's a relaxed little place that played a starring role in the founding of Canada, since it was the site of the first conference on Confederation in 1864. (P.E.I. opted out of joining when Confederation took place in 1867.)

The town is a good starting point for a cycle tour of the province if you haven't got all the gear you want. For rentals and advice, visit Gordon MacQueen at 430 Queen Street, Charlottetown, P.E.I. C1A 4E8. The proprietor of **MacQueen's Bike Shop** can also arrange for on-road service. For information call or fax (800) 667–4583.

While in Charlottetown you can engage in a little time travel by visiting ❖ **Beaconsfield Historic House,** in the city's poshest neighbourhood. This museum overlooks the harbor and the lieutenant governor's residence, Government House. Beaconsville is located at 2 Kent Street; you may find yourself driving around in circles if you don't hang a right after Richmond Street, thereby avoiding several one-way streets.

The home was built by a shipbuilder in 1877 at a cost of $50,000, at a time when decent annual salaries averaged $300. The three-and-a-half-story home features a double drawing room and nine decorative fireplaces, gaslight, and central heating. Faced with financial ruin after five short years, the original owners moved on.

Some of the original owner's creditors took it over, and when they couldn't sell it, they moved in. The new residents, the Cundalls, were a sober and dour lot. None of them married, and in 1916, when the last of them died, the home was turned into a "home for friendless young women" where they could get training in "useful arts." By 1935 it had become a student nurses' residence.

Beaconsfield Historic House

In the mid-1970s Beaconsfield became the headquarters of the Prince Edward Island Museum and Heritage Foundation. The home is now restored to the era when it was a private home, with period furniture and careful renovations. Even the little nursery is laid out as if the children had just been called away to supper.

Take a moment to look over the floor in the main hallway, made of painstakingly hand-laid tiles in an intricate mosaic pattern. The base of the spiral staircase has an original classic Greco-Roman statue lamp, converted from gas to electric. If you climb the stairs to the very top, you can enter the belvedere, an elegant enclosed lookout that offers beautiful views. Admission is $2.50.

Every Saturday during the summer there is an excellent **Ceilidh at the Irish Hall,** at 582 North River Road, featuring traditional Celtic song and dance by the Island's best traditional performers. For details call (902) 566–3273.

Also in Charlottetown, just about everyone loves the ◆ **Confederation Centre of the Arts**. In the summer of 1996, the production of *Anne of Green Gables* here will enter its thirty-second year of successful performances. It is the must-see show of The Island, quite possibly of the Maritimes.

Here you can also take in a free show of the young performers-in-training, in the outdoor amphitheater at noon in the summer. Other performances take place at 5:00 P.M. The **Young Company** presents shows such as *Spirit of the Nation,* which has been attended by more than 1,000 spectators at times. Seating is on steplike benches and the ground, so bring a pillow or other seating if you wish. Many of the young people in these shows end up with careers in the performing arts, so it's a good opportunity to see them in their fledgling roles.

For details call (800) 565–0278 within the Maritimes or (902) 566–1267; fax (902) 566–4648; or write to 145 Richmond Street, Charlottetown, P.E.I., C1A 1J1.

The Confederation Centre of the Arts also houses the largest art gallery and museum east of Montreal, with more than 15,000 works in the permanent collection. To find the complex, head to downtown Charlottetown via Queen Street. The arts center is left onto Richmond Street, a block before the harbor. It is wheelchair accessible.

If you decided to pass up Charlottetown for more rural delights, or if you wanted to leave the capital until you've worked your way fully around the circle, exit Dalvay onto Route 6, but then turn left onto Route 2. (You will still take this route if you head east from Charlottetown.)

Turn right at **Mount Stewart** onto St. Peter's Road, and just 2 miles (3.2 km) after this is the small community of **St. Andrews.** Here you'll find "The Little Church That's Been to Town and Back," a historic chapel built in 1803 at what is now called the ◆ **Bishop MacEachern National Historic Site.**

St. Andrew's Chapel was built by the Scottish settlers who had immigrated in 1772. It was the first major church on The Island, but by 1862 it was abandoned in favor of a larger building. Then, two years later the congregation embarked on a strange undertaking: With the help of 500 men and 50 teams of horses, the old church was placed on runners and hoisted onto a frozen river to be floated down to Charlottetown. As the little church approached the thin ice of the channel, disaster struck. The building crashed through the ice. With considerable effort the church was dragged out of the water and landed on Pownall Street. There it served as a girls' school for more than one hundred years.

The church was returned to the village in 1990, following a fire that destroyed some additions but left much of the original structure intact. To achieve this second move, the building was cut into four pieces and mounted on a flatbed truck. Now back in its former home, the fully restored church is a fine example of eighteenth-century Georgian architecture, which at the time of its original construction was much in use by the early settlers from England and Scotland.

The round-headed windows that you will see were discovered during the restoration and refurbishing that followed the near-destruction of the little church by fire in 1987.

The church is designated the Bishop MacEachern National Historic Site because it shares its site with the mausoleum of the revered Bishop MacEachern, who oversaw its original construction in 1803. As a young priest Father MacEachern proved his mettle by ministering to a flock that spread as far afield as New Brunswick. To cover his vast territory on the rudimentary roads, he resorted to snowshoes, skates, horseback, and, finally, a vehicle that combined the features of carriage, boat, and sled. This unusual conveyance can still be found at **St. Joseph's Convent** in Charlottetown.

The "Friends of St. Andrews" is a community group that administers the restored church. They hold concerts from time to time, so it is a good idea to ask about upcoming events at the reception desk. The Friends of St. Andrew's can be reached by phone at the home of Mary McInnis: (902) 676–2045. The postal address is: The Friends of St. Andrew's, P.O. Box 1864, Charlottetown, P.E.I. CIA 7N5.

Although the eastern end of the province is not geared up for large numbers of tourists, there are some nice campsites and charming bed-and-breakfast inns. In the area of **St. Peter's Bay** is the **Needles and Haystacks Bed and Breakfast.** This is inland rather than on the shore, but its central location offers some advantages to golfers, outdoors-people, and fans of the fiddle. The B&B is about 15 miles (25 km) away from the Links at Crowbush Cove Golf Course and about twenty minutes away from Brudenell Golf Course.

To get there drive inland on Route 2 from St. Peter's until you get to Dingwell's Mills, where you will turn right onto Route 4 and continue to Albion Cross. Make a left on Highway 327; a sign will soon direct you to the inn.

The big yellow home with dormers and bay windows dates back to the 1880s and is furnished with antiques. For years, before the passing away of proprietor Fred Foster's wife, Betty, one could witness traditional quiltmaking in the house. The finished quilts are still there.

The hospitality remains. Fred Foster plays an active role in the community and is a good source for information on local events. Nearby, he notes, are several good outings for Celtic music fans. The annual **Rollo Bay Fiddle Festival,** held the third weekend in July, is a short drive away. "It's a blast," says Fred. "People just have a great time, and a lot of Cape Breton fiddlers come over, too."

Rates for the inn are standard. Call (800) 563–2928.

The **Crab 'n' Apple Bed and Breakfast** is a quaint home on four acres (1½ hectares) of property overlooking St. Peter's Bay. It offers golf packages and has very reasonable rates. For information write to Richard Renaud and Seana Evans-Renaud, Box 9, St. Peter's Bay, P.E.I. C0A 2A0; phone (902) 961–3165.

Along with quiet walks through the fields and woods, you have the opportunity in this area to go on a deep-sea fishing charter. Just after St. Peter's Bay, a few miles up the coast, is a cozy little harbor, **Naufrage,** which is French for "shipwreck." It is a rustic harbor, complete with picturesque cliffs and lighthouse, a tiny river flowing through the middle of the cove, and a sandy beach.

There are a number of options for fishing in this end of The Island. At **North Lake** are several charter operations: **Mac's Deep Sea Fishing Inc.,** with Captain Malcolm Allen, at (902) 583–2568; the **North Lake Tuna Charters Inc.** at (902) 357–2055; or **Robertson's Tuna and Deep-Sea Fishing,** at (902) 357–2029.

If you decide to use North Lake as your point of departure for a fishing expedition, you may prefer to stay in St. Peter's Bay.

WHERE THE TIDES MEET

Now, continuing along the coast on Route 16, turn left at East Point and drive a short distance to the easternmost point of The Island and the 64-foot **East Point Lighthouse.** Energetic visitors who opt to climb to the top will be rewarded with a view of the swirling tides as the waves from the Northumberland Strait meet and crash against the surf of the Gulf of Saint Lawrence. Ask the guides for the lowdown on what to look for before you take the climb.

The coastline here has been so heavily eroded by the action of the waves that the lighthouse tower has been moved twice, including after the shipwreck of a British warship. This lighthouse was built in 1867 and is one of the oldest on the island. Admission is $2.50 for adults. Phone (902) 687–2295 for details. Kids age 6 and up are $1.00. Under 6, admission is free.

After viewing the lighthouse head back to East Point. Take a left turn onto Route 16 southbound until you get to the **South Lake** junction. This isn't really a lake at all. It's an estuary, an arm of the gulf that is also fed by a source of fresh water. The owners of the ✦**Arrowhead Lodge** explain that the water there is bathtub warm. Incidentally, it's just after the South Lake sign that you'll see a sign for Arrowhead Lodge. Turn left here and follow the private road until it terminates at the lodge. The lodge is a new place, set on more than thirty acres (12 hectares) of unspoiled nature, fronting on the lake. When the property was being prepared for building, the owners unearthed a number of native arrowheads, hence the name of the lodge. They've provided a lot of special touches in the lodge, like a pool table and a high-powered telescope for watching the wildlife from the second-floor lounge area.

With only three luxury guest rooms, the lodge caters to travelers looking to get away from it all. Each suite has a king-size bed, big old-fashioned bathtub, and fireplace. Rates range from moderate to deluxe. To reserve call (902) 357–2482.

At South Lake is the junction of Route 16A. At this point turn right to drive to **Elmira** to visit the ✦**Elmira Railway Museum.**

The museum is located next to the endpoint of the **Confederation Trail.** This trail was converted from the railroad line when train service was shut down on The Island. The portion in this area was the section chosen for the pilot project. All along this beautiful nature trail are rest stops in converted train stations. The pathways are slated to be resurfaced so smoothly that they will be wheelchair accessible.

As tiny as The Island is, the railway boom of the last century played an important role in P.E.I. history. Remember that although there was a conference on Confederation in Prince Edward Island in 1864, Islanders decided not to join the union of Nova Scotia, New Brunswick, Ontario, and Quebec in 1867. They feared that their voice would be overwhelmed by the much greater numbers of voters elsewhere.

By 1870 however, "railway fever" hit The Island in a big way. Islanders were convinced that a railroad would bring new factories, easier access to markets for farmers, and prosperity to every doorstep. Soon every village wanted to be connected to the main line and the rails zigzagged across The Island like top-stitching on a crazy quilt.

In short order the railway ran up an unmanageable debt. The Island government was unable to pay its lenders, mostly British banks, and by 1872 a series of railway scandals had toppled it. The Canadian Confederation offered to take over the debt and provide railway service under its administration, in exchange for P.E.I. becoming part of Canada—hence the name Confederation Trail.

All this and more are explained at Elmira Railway Museum. The rustic entranceway to the trail is just to your right as you approach the Elmira Railway Museum's reception center. In the winter you can cross-country ski the same route that you pass over by bicycle or foot in the summer.

The museum is set in the eastern terminus of the railway. Finished in 1912, it was the last station built. It has telegraph equipment that is still in working condition; there are also fare books, schedules, and artifacts from days gone by. The station office looks exactly as it must have looked when the railway was still being run in the British colonial tradition: Gentlemen and ladies had separate waiting rooms, since, the guide explains, "The men would spit into the spittoons and curse and shock the ladies." After Canadian National took over, separate waiting rooms became a thing of the past, and ladies were free to be as shocked as they pleased. Admission is $1.50.

From here turn back onto Route 16A, then right onto Route 16, and continue driving south in the direction of **Basin Head.** This is a great spot for photography buffs and birdwatchers. The area boasts the ✦ **Basin Head Fisheries Museum,** constructed on a headland overlooking one of The Island's finest white-sand beaches. The sand here is so pure that it squeaks when you walk on it. Even on a sizzling day in August there will hardly be a person on this perfect, out-of-the-way beach.

The museum depicts the transition of Prince Edward Island's inshore fishery. By now you will have noticed the large number of "farmed fish" on The Island; fish farming has grown into a thriving segment of P.E.I.'s fishery. Here you can also tour a one-time fish cannery that now houses a coastal exhibit.

The museum is open from the beginning of July to Labour Day, from 10:00 A.M. to 5:00 P.M. daily. In June and September it closes earlier, at 3:00 P.M., and is closed Monday, Tuesday, and Saturday. A small admission fee is charged.

After Basin Head you will head south in the direction of **Souris.** If time allows and you feel like a country walk, you can take in a Heritage road—one of The Island's prettiest—by making a small detour. To do this, when you reach **Little Harbour,** turn right off Route 16 onto Route 303, also known as the New Harmony Road. From there continue to Greenvale.

A small clay road connects Greenvale Road to the Tarantum Road (also known as Route 304) for a distance of about ¾ mile (1.6 km). Sunlight peeks through a lush canopy created by a mixture of hardwoods and softwoods and falls on the brilliant green of thick vegetation and the hardened clay of the old road. On the eastern side of this road, the Provincial Department of Energy and Forestry operates a **demonstration woodlot** that is open to the public.

During Prohibition years the isolation of the canopied road made it a favorite haunt of rumrunners who used the area to stash illegal cargo.

Souris is also the ferry terminal for the boat to the Magdalen Islands, so the town always has a flow of visitors passing through during the summer. Incidentally, the name Souris comes from the French word for "mouse." In the early to mid-1700s, plagues of field mice overran the settlement, giving the place its unusual name.

A nice place to stay in Souris is **The Matthew House Inn,** which features Victorian art and antique furniture, four fireplaces (nice for cozy breakfasts), and an exercise room, complete with sauna. The spacious Victorian boasts two libraries, including one with a fireplace and a vintage video library for those nights when you just want to warm your toes by the fire.

The inn was once the home of Uriah Matthew, a partner in Matthew, McLean and Company, which operated the village's general store, the harbor wharf, and a fleet of thirty fishing boats, as well as a lobster company and shipping operation that sent goods as far afield as the West Indies. The family of the original owners has allowed the innkeepers to retain the Victoria-era paintings, which add to the nostalgic appeal of this charming getaway.

You can't miss it if you look for the Magdalen Islands Ferry, which is a stone's throw away. You will find it harborside on 15 Breakwater Street. Call (902) 687–3461 for reservations. Rates are standard.

Just outside of Souris, on Route 2, is **Rollo Bay.** Each summer, on the third weekend in July, lovers of traditional fiddle music can have a great time at the **Rollo Bay Fiddle Festival,** which features talent from all over North America. The big attraction is fiddle music, including traditional Celtic violin strathbanes, jigs, and reels in open-air settings, including old-time dances.

Just south of Rollo Bay, you'll come to a fork in the road that leads to **Bay Fortune.** Turn onto Route 310. Here you will find ◆ **The Inn at Bay Fortune,** reputed to be the home of one of the two best restaurants on The Island (the other great meal being at Dalvay-by-the-Sea). Count on spending $50 per person for dinner. You must reserve a table, due to the reputation of its chef, American Michael Smith, formerly of Tiffanys on the Bay in New York City, The Brass Parrot at the Buccaneer in St. Croix in the U.S. Virgin Islands, and the winner of numerous honors. He's a tall, lanky windsurfer, which explains his annual pilgrimage to Bay Fortune's windy shores.

If you would like to learn how to create such culinary wizardry for yourself, you can take a course here from the master chef himself. The **Inn Style Cooking Classes** involve two days of intensive study, including a culinary tour of gardens, fields, and forest for ingredient gathering and guidance on the nuances of tasting while preparing a meal. The course includes supper on both nights of the course and costs $225, with special rates available for two or more people. For details call (902) 687–3745 in the summer or 860–296–1348 in the winter, or write to The Inn at Bay Fortune, Souris, P.E.I., C0A 2B0.

Apart from the gourmet delights, the inn is a cozy place with an interesting history. It was the former summer home of playwright Elmer Harris, who wrote the 1940s play *Johnny Belinda*. After this was a huge success on Broadway, it was made into a movie. The playwright's summer home was a writers' colony where many of his friends summered and wrote. Eventually it became the home of actress Colleen Dewhurst, who is well known for her role as Marilla in the television series *Anne of Green Gables*. She was the wife of George C. Scott, whose son was married here.

When the beloved actress died of cancer a few years ago, her summer home was made over into an inn. The place has eleven guest rooms and a lovely view of the bay. Rates are moderate. For reservations call (902) 687–3745.

HILLS AND HARBORS

After enjoying Bay Fortune continue south along Route 2 until you reach Dingwells Mills, where you'll turn left onto Route 4 and continue to Pooles Corner. Then turn left onto Route 3 and continue until you reach the ❦ **Brudenell River Provincial Park.**

This park has quite a lot to offer in the way of pleasant diversions: trail rides, canoe and kayaking adventures, a championship-level golf course, a riverside beach, and a marina for water sports. If camping is not your style, there is a collection of chalets along the river, although they seem quite small and boxlike and lacking in privacy. Organized activities emphasize the natural setting, with walking trails that will take you along pathways lined with wildflowers or through marshland. Bike paths lead to Georgetown and Cardigan, at 5 and 7 miles (or 7 and 11 km) distance respectively, with the Cardigan path traversing the old rail-line-turned-Confederation Trail.

The golf course at **Brudenell** has been host to four national and six Canadian Professional Golf Association tournaments. Its pristine riverside setting, immaculate greens, and tree-lined fairways offer a challenge to golfers of all levels. Greens fees are $30, with a discount for seniors and a twilight rate of just $18, which will allow you to play long into the warm summer evenings.

At Brudenell you can rent horses and go on a romantic, not to mention scenic, trail ride along the beach at sunset, or even an overnight ride, accompanied by an experienced guide. These are available through reservation only; call (902) 652–2396. There are several other exciting diversions in this area, including an opportunity to go sea kayaking along secluded offshore islands and sandy coves.

The marina comes in handy if you are interested in taking a look at a harbor-seal colony. **Cruise Manada,** run by Captain Dan Bear, departs from either the Montague Marina or the Brudenell Marina at various times throughout the day. Along with the cruise, Bear takes his passengers to a mussel farm where The Island's famous Atlantic Blue mussels are grown. The whole trip takes two and a quarter hours. If you are lucky, you may see a whale, harbor porpoise, or osprey in addition to the many sea birds in the area. The cruise costs $13.50 for adults, with discounts for senior and children. More information can be had by calling (902) 838–3444.

Stay at nearby Montague or try camping at **Panmure Island.** To get to Panmure Island Provincial Park, drive east along Route 17 from Montague. Panmure Island offers two different kinds of beaches: a beach fronting on St. Mary's Bay, and one open to the gulf. Set in a lovely pastoral area, the view of the ocean and the spaciousness of the hundred-acre campground are a bargain, with camping fees starting at $12.50 daily. For more information on this or other camping areas in the eastern end of the Island, write to P.O. Box 370, Montague, P.E.I. C0A 1R0; or call at (902) 652–2356.

Where do the buffalo roam these days? If you're on Prince Edward Island, this wouldn't seem to be a likely question, but you will find a herd of buffalo at ◆ **Buffaloland Provincial Park,** just 3¾ miles (6 km) south of Montague on Highway 4.

In May 1970 fifteen young buffalo arrived on The Island as a gift from Saskatchewan to the government of P.E.I. It was just a small herd then, but nature has taken care of that. At last count there were about sixty or seventy of the animals.

The buffalo are cared for by John Nicholson, who was eighty-six years old in 1995. He formerly owned the one hundred-acre (40-hectare) piece of land where they graze, and he now acts as caretaker of the herd, being the person they are most comfortable with. But "I still have to be very careful around them," he notes.

He used to take his truck right in among the herd to feed them but now feeds them through the fence. The park is bisected by a long, fenced-in column that people can walk down to get a feeling of being surrounded by a herd of wild buffalo. There is also a platform accessed by steps, which makes it possible to look out over the herd.

Calves are born in May or June. Periodically, the herd has to be culled. On these occasions the animals designated for slaughter are put out to tender, according to park inspector Bill Buell. "Generally the same groups bid for the animals," he said, including Micmac natives who prize the meat. The day I visited several carloads of Micmacs from Nova Scotia were there to take a look. They had just been to the big annual Abegweit Pow-Wow at Panmure Island.

A herd of buffalo is something to see in the spring, when the animals are in heat. The elder bull buffalo make a circle around the females to protect them at the first sign of humans dropping by to take a look. If you get too close to the fence, they'll charge right at you and ram into the fence, which didn't look like a very sturdy defense.

Interpretive signs explain details of the life of the buffalo. On sunny days it takes a lot to coax them out from under the trees at the back of the park, so if you have time and want to see the buffalo at their best, pick an overcast morning or early evening that's not too hot. Admission to Buffaloland is free.

Next drive southeast to **Murray Harbour,** a nice, out-of-the-way fishing community. When you reach Murray River cross the bridge and then exit left onto Route 18 in the direction of Murray Harbour.

There are several things to see in this area, including the ◆ **Log Cabin Museum.** It's located on Route 18A, the exit for which is just before you reach the village.

This privately owned museum houses antiques dating back 200 years as well as a collection of still-operable phonographs, including Edison cylinder machines dating from 1895 and 1905 and a 1905 RCA Victor. The owner of the museum demonstrates the old phonographs, playing a cylindrical record of Harry Lawton, an English singer from the turn of the century. The more recent record player was shown off with a record from the '40s: Patty Page singing "How Much is That Doggie in the Window?"

73

The impressive group of antiques was assembled by a private collector named Preston Robertson, who had to keep building additions onto the original log cabin in order to house his ever-growing collection. Another large log structure extends out the back to contain his sleighs and buggies. Of these, his prize is a restored, 135-year-old sleigh. Robertson said that it takes him an average of two months to restore each sleigh or buggy. When I visited he was busy fixing up a new acquisition.

Murray Harbour itself is a good point of departure for nature tours. From here you can experience sea kayaking along the shoreline for excursions ranging from half a day to three or five days. One tour centers on the islands of Murray Harbour. You'll not only see the double-crested cormorants on Cherry Island, but get to experience the isolation of secluded areas of unspoiled coastline.

Murray Harbour also has a good seal-watching opportunity in the form of ◆ **Captain Garry's Seal and Bird Watching Cruises.** During July and August a skipper by the improbably appropriate name of Captain Garry Herring takes his passengers to see the largest seal colony on The Island and to Bird Island to see thousands of cormorants, blue herons, arctic terns, and bald eagles. The cost for adults is $13.50; for children it's $7.00. For details call (800) 561–2494.

A quaint bed-and-breakfast establishment in the neighborhood of Murray River is **Bayberry Cliff Inn,** on Route 4, Little Sands, a few minutes' drive from the ferry terminal. This place overlooks a cliff, giving a spectacular view of the ocean, with five different levels and a number of sitting areas and balconies.

The owners are Nancy and Don Perkins. Nancy is a local marine painter whose creations are on sale in local galleries as well as at the nearby **Rossignol Estate Winery,** where fruit wines are produced and sold.

Nancy is a big fan of twig furniture. The inn's front porch and yard are full of chairs made out of tree branches, complete with birdhouses and other bits of over-the-top whimsy. The house itself was originally a barn, which they converted over an eleven-year period after moving it to its cliffside location.

Room rates are standard, with weekly rates available. For more information call (902) 962–3395.

At this point you are within minutes of a ferry to Nova Scotia, but if you want to linger another day on The Island, continue for a half hour on TCH Route 1, the same stretch of the TransCanada Highway that passes in front of the ferry terminal.

You will come to a sign indicating the ❖ **Orwell Corner Historic Village,** reached by taking a right turn after the junction of Routes 1 and 23, up a small hill and at the start of a clay road. This site re-creates the life and times of a small crossroads agricultural village from the last century. The village includes a farmhouse from 1864, a smithy, and a shingle mill, which I haven't seen anywhere else in the Maritimes. Timing is a factor here: If you come on a Wednesday, you'll be able to take part in a really good *ceilidh,* one of the best of these traditional Gaelic parties on The Island. Events during the harvest and Christmas seasons make the village particularly picturesque. For details of upcoming events, call (902) 368–6600.

The village operates cooperatively with the nearby restored homestead of one of Prince Edward Island's most noteworthy citizens. Sir Andrew Macphail was a physician and professor at McGill University in Montreal. He was also an author intensely interested in sustainable agricultural and forestry development. At age fifty he volunteered to work with a field ambulance corps in World War I. He was knighted by the King on New Year's Day 1918.

His birthplace is now called the **Sir Andrew Macphail Homestead,** a 140-acre (56-hectare) site, with a reforestation project including a tree nursery, and wildlife gardens. A nature trail meanders along the side of a stream. Visitors can dine or have tea in the facilities provided in the restored home, which also boasts a large conference room in the former dining room. Dinner is quite reasonably priced, and the restaurant is licensed to serve alcohol.

From Orwell Corner you can backtrack in the direction of the Wood Island ferry. There is just one more thing that you ought to do to make your Prince Edward Island sojourn complete: Turn left off of TransCanada Highway Route One onto Route 209 and visit ❖ **Point Prim Lighthouse.**

This is a charming little peninsula that seems like a little world unto itself. You can visit the lighthouse here and just to the west of it, the ❖ **Lighthouse Artist Gallery and Chowder House.**

Of all the old lighthouses on The Island, the Point Prim dates back the furthest, to 1845. The 60-foot tower is the only round brick lighthouse in the entire country. You can climb inside to the polygonal lantern house and catch a spectacular bird's-eye view of Northumberland Strait while you check your pulse.

Once you've worked up an appetite, drop by the Chowder House and try the Irish moss pudding. In other parts of P.E.I., when recipes are made with this ingredient, they call it seaweed. But the owner of the Chowder House hates it when you call it seaweed, because it's not really seaweed. (You can also buy some dried Irish moss to take home for your own culinary experiments.) I leave this tour of P.E.I. with the restaurant's house recipe for Irish Moss Pudding so that you can share it with your friends back home:

Lighthouse Artist Gallery and Chowder House
Irish Moss Pudding

⅓ cup Irish moss (packed)
4 cups milk
¼ tsp. salt
1½ tsp. vanilla

Soak moss for 15 minutes in enough water to cover, drain. Pick over the Irish moss, removing the undesirable pieces. Add moss to milk and cook in the double boiler for 30 minutes. Add salt and vanilla. Pour through a sieve. Fill molds and chill. Serve with a fruit topping.

NOVA SCOTIA'S ATLANTIC COASTLINE

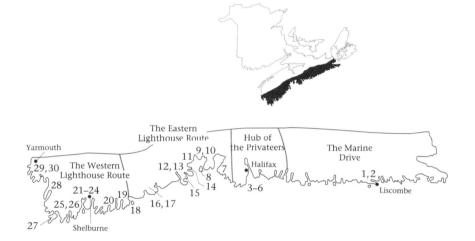

1. Sherbrooke
2. Liscomb Lodge
3. International Busker's Festival
4. The Citadel
5. Birdland
6. Public Gardens
7. Peggy's Cove
8. Tancook Islands
9. Captain's House Inn
10. The Chester Playhouse
11. Oak Island
12. Mahone Bay
13. Craftspeople
14. Fisheries Museum of the Atlantic
15. The Ovens
16. Perkins House
17. Queens County Museum
18. The Quarterdeck Beachside Villas and Grill
19. Seaside Adjunct
20. Port l'Herbert Pocket Wilderness
21. Ross–Thomson House
22. Cooper's Inn
23. Shelburne County Museum
24. The Dory Shop
25. Barrington Woolen Mill
26. Old Meeting House in Barrington
27. Clark's Harbour
28. Musée Acadien
29. Firefighter's Museum
30. Yarmouth County Museum

Nova Scotia's Atlantic Coastline

If you have followed the routing outlined in this book to explore the Maritimes, you will have entered Prince Edward Island from New Brunswick and exited P.E.I. via Nova Scotia.

As such, you will no sooner arrive in Nova Scotia then you will be pointed toward Cape Breton, a route commonly followed by travelers to the area. This often leads to an unfortunate bypass of much of the Northumberland Strait coast of Nova Scotia. Although there are few historic highlights in this region, that is not to say that there are none. There are also a number of wonderful beach areas along the Northumberland Strait. Marked on the Travelways maps distributed by the Ministry of Tourism and Culture, these areas are among those I encourage you to explore at your leisure.

If you travel directly to Cape Breton, take the TransCanada Highway 104, which travels along the Northumberland shoreline, and return from Cape Breton on the Atlantic coastline, in the little-traveled county of Guysborough. By following this route you'll see much of the province's mainland's unspoiled rural charm.

The Marine Drive

One Guysborough highlight must be a visit to the town of 🔷 **Sherbrooke,** which, starting in the 1860s, was the site of a massive gold rush that went on for twenty years until it suddenly collapsed. The remains of those days are a collection of thirty perfectly preserved buildings fronting on the beautiful St. Mary's River. These include a school, drug store, courthouse, blacksmith's shop, and barn (complete with horses). House after house is filled with artifacts from the town's "golden era."

Costumed guides explain the history of Nova Scotia's gold rush. The economic activity of Nova Scotia gold rushes of the last century produced an income higher than that of the Klondike gold rush. Several old mines are still around in the province, and a few are reopening thanks to modern technology.

If you are eager to spend more time in this area, you can find cabins, some overlooking the rapids of St. Mary's River, at 🔷 **Liscomb Lodge.** The lodge offers an indoor pool and a fitness center, as well as access to a wide range of outdoor sporting equipment and guides. (There are nature trails and nesting eagles nearby.) For reservations call (800) 665–6343. Rates are deluxe.

If you're just passing through, you might want to drop by the restaurant to enjoy a bite or to check out the dozens of locally handmade quilts and other crafts that adorn the post-and-beam ceiling of the main lodge's second floor. These items are for sale.

HUB OF THE PRIVATEERS

They don't teach this in local history lessons, but the truth is, piracy was big business in Nova Scotia once the British got hold of the territory. After hostilities broke out with the renegade colonies to the south, Britain took full advantage of the colony's strategic position and commissioned all sorts of ships for "privateering," which was piracy by all intents and purposes. Young men signed on with privateers as a way of avoiding being "press-ganged" into service with the notoriously brutal Royal Navy. Add to this the fact that Britain was almost constantly at war with somebody or other and you can see that the high seas represented a tremendous career opportunity for the adventurous sort with a strong stomach. Captured booty was taken to Halifax where it was "libelled off" in public auctions, and the proceeds split between the shipowners, the court, and government officials.

It was this piracy and war that really gave Halifax a leg up. Even the cobblestones of the city's first streets were quarried from the shattered ruins of Fortress Louisbourg, which fell to the British shortly before Halifax's founding. Some areas of downtown Halifax still contain these stones, such as the Granville Street entrance to the Art College.

But after the War of 1812 drew to a close, piracy was no longer government-endorsed.

Halifax's waterfront is still a fun place to hang out, pirates or no, since the city boasts a lively music scene, excellent shopping for local arts and crafts, and gourmet seafood.

Driven by the demands of six universities full of students, the nightlife can be relaxed, fun, and easy on the wallet. For both visitors and locals, the focus of interest stretches from Argyle Street, a few blocks from the harbor, to Historic Properties, with its restored waterfront buildings from the last century. Early each August the

79

❖ **International Busker's Festival** draws street entertainers from around the world.

Overlooking the city, the fortress to which the city owes its birth ❖ **The Citadel,** provides a stunning lookout. **Point Pleasant Park** is an extensive rustic park at the tip of Halifax's posh south end. The city also boasts large, traditional English-style gardens.

Opinions about Halifax are as varied as the people who live here. Unself-conscious, or perhaps totally lacking in pretense, is the best way to describe it. When an article in *Harper's Bazaar* cited the place as the next cool city in North America after Seattle's grunge thing, everyone in Halifax had a good laugh. Halifax cool? Can't be. And yet, the city is an eclectic mix that somehow manages to be avant-garde.

The downtown is full of funky little cafes decorated with original paintings and folk art, the epitome of which must be the Soho Kitchen on Granville Street. The cafe culture is no doubt a byproduct of the downtown Nova Scotia College of Art and Design. Called NSCAD by locals, the school was founded by the one-time governess of the King of Siam's children, Anna Leonowens, whose day job was immortalized in the movie *The King and I.* For many years NSCAD was the only degree-granting art college in Canada.

NSCAD has left an indelible stamp on the funky downtown core of Halifax, as has the city's seafaring past. The Privateer's Wharf and the shops down by the waterfront are converted old-time warehouses from the Age of Sail. You are as likely to hear an avant-garde band perform original music that has won fans from all over Canada as you are to watch a crowd of Maritimers pouring onto the dance floor to the tune of "What Shall We Do With the Drunken Sailor," a traditional Halifax jig if ever there was one.

Currently, the most trendy place to go out is ❖ **Birdland,** situated near the Chateau Halifax hotel. Bands that perform at Birdland often have recording contracts and large college followings. The crowd is decidedly twenty-something.

Where to go when in Halifax? If you arrive during the day, gravitate toward the beautiful ❖ **Public Gardens,** and from there meander along Spring Garden Road toward the harbor.

Between these two points, you will find countless coffee shops, all manner of restaurants, pubs, and chip wagons, grunge-clad teens, bohemian types, college students, and out-of-towners.

The 17-acre (7-hectare) Public Gardens were originally created as a private garden begun in 1753, only four years after the founding of Halifax. In 1836 they were taken over by the Nova Scotia Horticultural Society. Since 1889 the park has been enclosed by a wrought-iron fence, punctuated by an ornate pair of ornamental gates imported from Glasgow, Scotland.

The gardens are now recognized as the finest original formal Victorian gardens in North America. They have rhododendrons so massive that you can walk under a huge canopy of leaves, hidden from the passersby on the other side. The duck pond in the middle of the garden leads into a stream, lined with irises and day lilies, that passes under a small arching stone bridge. Swans share the pond with the ducks, and if you arrive at a propitious time of year, you may catch glimpses of baby swans and little ducklings dutifully swimming after their mothers.

Along with the carefully tended roses, there are floating-style flower beds in French Formal and English Romantic styles. The Victorian bandstand in the center of the park is the site of free concerts on Sunday afternoons.

Across Sackville Street, which borders the gardens on the north side, you will see greenhouses. Next to them a charming stone house, Public Gardens Cottage, dates back to the life and times of Richard Power, one-time gardener to the duke of Devonshire in Ireland. His descendants tended the gardens until the 1960s. During the summer months a tourist bureau is operated there (designated by the large **?** on the city map).

For a small city, ethnic food abounds, with lots of Lebanese, Italian, Greek, Vietnamese, Thai, and East Indian as well as vegetarian places awaiting your discovery. Later in the evening embark on a pub crawl, a sport heavily favored by the city's many university students.

THE EASTERN LIGHTHOUSE ROUTE

Take a Canadian 10-cent piece in your hand and examine the sailing ship that enjoys equal billing with Her Majesty the Queen. That is the famous Nova Scotia sailing ship, the *Bluenose,* as photographed by W. R. MacAskill. For two decades during the early part of this century, this schooner won one international race after another. Eventually, it came to symbolize the pride of

Canada's seagoing Easterners. A replica of the *Bluenose* graces the Halifax harbor today.

The photographer whose famous shot found its way to the Canadian dime also made famous another Nova Scotian landmark: ◆ **Peggy's Cove.** This once-isolated fishing cove has become so synoymous with "quaint fishing villages" that it has become anything *but* off the beaten path. Now busloads of tourists come to soak in the "unspoiled beauty" of this village.

Those who consider a pilgrimage to Peggy's Cove mandatory do themselves a disservice if they do not continue farther down the **South Shore** to the historic villages and other unspoiled and largely untouched coastal communities along Highway 3, which is provincially designated the "Lighthouse Route."

During the colonial era the British Crown supplied Nova Scotian privateers with letters of marque, entitling them to loot and plunder enemy ships. This freewheeling approach to the seafaring tradition was revived during the era of Prohibition, when rum-runners smuggled contraband booze into the United States from the tiny fishing communities that dot the South Shore. From the south end of Halifax to the southernmost tip of the province, some of the grandest old homes had their beginnings as the houses of sea captains who owed their wealth to their success on the high seas and hidden coves.

To reach the South Shore from Halifax, follow the "shore road," also known as Route 333, which will give you a glimpse of the many unspoiled coastal communities, like **Seabright, French Village,** and **Indian Harbour,** that line **St. Margarets Bay.** You can also drop by Peggy's Cove if you really have to take a look. If you want to bypass this area and get into the South Shore more directly, take Provincial Highway 103, which you can also access from Route 333 at Exit 5. At this point you will have reached the head of St. Margarets Bay.

City dwellers looking for a good beach often head to this bay because it is shallow and runs sufficiently far back that the water is reasonably warm in late summer. Several beaches that offer excellent swimming are in **Hubbards** and **Queensland.**

If you follow along Route 329, you'll reach the point of the peninsula that separates St. Margaret's Bay from **Mahone Bay.** Here you will also find a provincial picnic park and Bayswater

The *Bluenose* II in Halifax Harbor

Beach, with its broad stretch of white sand. From time to time seals can be seen sunning themselves nearby.

The name Mahone actually is derived from the French word *mahonne,* which was the kind of vessel favored by French pirates. Foremost among the bay's islands are **Big** and **Little ⬧ Tancook Islands,** with populations of permanent residents numbering 218 and thirty-two respectively. The islands can be reached by a small, pedestrian-only ferry that runs four times daily during the week, more frequently on the weekends. Details on the ferry can be had by phoning Tancook Island Transportation at (902) 228–2340. Avoid taking the last ferry of the day to Tancook if you want to return the same day, since it docks on the island for the night.

The first European settlers on the islands were German farmers who settled on the islands because they could let their cattle range freely. They soon discovered that the soil was perfect for growing oversize cabbages; even today Tancook is noted for its superb sauerkraut. You can't miss it in local grocery stores. It is imaginatively labeled "Tancook Sauerkraut" and comes packaged in something resembling a red-and-white-striped milk carton.

The permanent residents are now most commonly involved in the fishing industry; historically they engaged in schooner-building. In addition to the company of seagulls, the thrill of isolation in a completely out-of-the-way seaside setting, and nature trails, Big Tancook Island offers a bed and breakfast, a canteen, a grocery store, and a gift shop.

Two colorful villages overlook Mahone Bay. On three fingers of one peninsula you will find **Chester,** which was, from its beginning, a hub of privateer raids. Its first residents were transplanted Bostonians, in 1759. These were followed by United Empire Loyalists, along with French, Germans, and Swiss.

Its early links to New England did not spare Chester from being the focus of raids by American privateers. In 1782, while the village's men were off gathering firewood, three such ships threatened to sack the defenseless village. The broomstick-carrying women of the village marched back and forth along the hill above the community, the red linings of their cloaks worn outward. The privateers, thinking that the village was guarded by British redcoats, decided to sail farther south and sack neighboring Lunenburg instead.

In the early part of the 1800s, the village was the summer home of the Reverend John Secombe, an American, whose home is now the landmark ♦ **Captain's House Inn** on Central Street. This offers overnight accommodations as well as fine dining, with a back deck providing a good view of Front Harbour. Advance reservations are a good idea if you plan to stay during the summer months. Phone (902) 275–3501. Prices are standard.

Throwing a stone from the back deck of this inn could probably shatter one of the colorful platters or bowls made by folk artist Jim Smith, who operates **Nova Scotia Folk Pottery** on Front Harbour during the summer months. Also in Chester you can shop for quality woven crafts, such as quilts and linens, at the **Warp and Woof** on Water Street.

For the past hundred years or so, Chester has been the discreet summer retreat of sailing enthusiasts, from the descendants of U.S. president Grover Cleveland to the presidents of universities, along with a smattering of cabinet ministers, former prime minister Pierre Trudeau, and famous authors like Mordecai Richler.

The affluent summer crowd swells the village's permanent population of 1,000 by as much as 30 percent, giving it both a touch of cultural vibrancy and the lotus-eater quality of exotic haunts. There are gleaming yachts and Jaguars, Mercedeses, seaside eateries with trendy menus, and Cape Cod architecture without the New York crowd. Yet few people even in neighboring Halifax give Chester a second thought except during **Race Week,** which since 1904 has been the culmination of the social season.

The race draws sailors from Boston and beyond, filling the bay with sleek yachts. Parties spring up everywhere, and people flock to ❖ **The Chester Playhouse.** This was recently purchased and then donated to the village by financier and author Christopher Ondaatje, who spends his summers on his hundred-acre (40-hectare) island in Mahone Bay. He summed up the reason for his generosity thusly: "None of the people who come here want to make a buck out of Chester."

A few years back the playhouse was enjoying enormous success presenting opera with puppets. Every summer something new and fresh keeps the regulars coming back. You can get a brochure outlining the program by writing The Chester Playhouse, P.O. Box 293, Chester, N.S. B0J 1J0, or by phoning (902) 275–3933.

Perhaps owing to the affluence of its summer visitors, the tiny village has a surprising number of eating establishments serving excellent seafood. You can also find a decidedly civilized breakfast at **Julien's Pastry Shop,** which specializes in croissants and cappuccino. Add to this the village's watering holes (the oldest and most popular of these is the Fo'c'sle), and you get the impression of an uncluttered corner of The Hamptons.

Farther along Provincial Highway 103, or closer to the shoreline, on Highway 3, you will pass ❖ **Oak Island,** reputed to be the site where Captain William Kidd hid his treasure. For two centuries people have risked their lives (and sometimes lost them) trying to get at the treasure hidden under an elaborate network of underground tunnels. Visitors can tour the site, where excavation is still ongoing.

Continuing along down Highway 103, you'll come to the community of ◆ **Mahone Bay,** which has several star attractions tucked in among this sailor's paradise and its bay with 360-odd islands.

As soon as you enter the community you'll see the village's star attraction: The pretty shoreline, dotted with churches, is a postcard waiting to happen. Pull into the **Inlet Cafe,** situated at the perfect bend in the road for photographing Mahone Bay. Set up your tripod or prop your camera on the stone retaining wall at the front of the cafe and you will get a picture of one of the most photogenic spots in the province.

This village gives the impression of being a bit busier than Chester, since a number of ◆ **craftspeople** have set up shop here.

This is a good place for antiques-hunting, and visitors can also visit pottery, pewter, and rug-hooking studios, and photo and art galleries. It seems that few can resist buying a quilt when they visit this area of Nova Scotia. And this area of the province is a great place to look for these. Foremost among the shops offering stunning patchwork apparel and quilts are **Suttles and Seawinds,** on Mahone Bay's Main Street. Nearby are two pottery shops of note: **Birdsall-Worthington Pottery Ltd.** has slip-decorated eathernware pottery and handmade earrings, while **K. R. Thompson** has soda-fired porcelain in sea-inspired greens and blues. Another shop worth a visit is the upscale **Teazer,** on Edgewater Drive, which is noted for fine local crafts and quality clothing.

Privateers figured prominently in the community's history. During the War of 1812, an American ship, *The Young Teazer* was chased into Mahone Bay by a British warship. One of the crew aboard the privateer was a British deserter who set fire to the ship's powder magazine rather than be captured by the British. The resulting explosion killed twenty-eight crewmen.

The flourishing shipbuilding trade of old-time Mahone Bay brought with it considerable wealth, as shown by the many stately old Victorian, Georgian, and Cape Cod homes here. Many Main Street businesses occupy buildings formerly used by shipbuilders. A "Walking Tour" brochure gives a closer look at the local architecture. It's available at the **Mahone Bay Settler's Museum,** on Main Street. On the last weekend in July, the village hosts a **wooden boat festival.**

The stretch along the coast from Chester to Mahone Bay is also a favorite area for cycle touring, since it offers picture-perfect coastline and frequent rest stops—in the way of seafood restaurants. Try the highly recommended **Ocean Grill** on South Main Street in Mahone Bay. Prices are moderate for its "fresh market and ocean cooking" style of food.

After Mahone Bay continue along Trunk Highway 3 until you reach **Lunenburg,** the birthplace of many famous ships. It was here that the *Bluenose* and its replica were built, as well as the full-scale replica of H.M.S. *Bounty* used in the Marlon Brando version of *Mutiny on the Bounty.*

As far as picturesque fishing villages go, they don't get any prettier than Lunenburg and its harbor, proof of which you will find on the back of a Canadian $100 bill. The scene hasn't changed a whit since the photograph on the bill was shot.

Most prominent of all the waterfront buildings is a large red building alongside a wharf. This is the ✦ **Fisheries Museum of the Atlantic.** Along with the aquarium and working dory shop, the museum has several fishing vessels, including the schooner *Theresa E. Connor.* This sailing ship, built in the 1930s, was used in the fisheries for twenty-five years. Here you get the opportunity to practice traditional fishermen's skills such as net repair and ropemaking. Since fishing was Lunenburg's lifeblood virtually from its founding, these traditions go way back and have stamped the area permanently with the lore and spirit of the people who make their living from the sea.

One of the big outcroppings of this is a strong tradition of folk music and art, as evidenced by the **Lunenburg Folk Harbour Festival,** held on the second weekend of August every year. This is a really great party, well worth timing your visit for, so keep it in mind.

There is also an annual **craft festival** in which many local artisans display their wares. It is timed to take place on the second weekend in July. Since the town is so pleasant and picturesque, many craftspeople and artists live in the vicinity, making this a good bet for people interested in buying or looking at some folk art or crafts.

In Lunenburg you can stay at the historic **Boscawen Inn,** built in 1888. It is located at 150 Cumberland Street, overlooking the harbor. Its seventeen guest rooms are furnished with antiques. Rates are standard for the inn, which has a 3½-star rating. The restaurant is also highly rated and participates in the "Taste of Nova Scotia" program. For reservations call (902) 634–3325 or write to Boscawen Inn, 150 Cumberland Street, Box 1343, Lunenburg, N.S. B0J 2C0.

The thing that really gave Lunenburg its color was the influx, at the time of its founding in 1753, of large numbers of German Protestants, by boat from Halifax. *Deutsch* (German) soon became "Dutch" in everyone's mind; soon everyone was calling them the Lunenburg Dutch. Their descendants have put an indelible stamp on the local lingo, strongly accented and with verbs that sometimes find their way to the end of the sentence, among other gems. If you meet a Nova Scotian nicknamed "Dutchy," you can bet he's from Lunenburg.

The German connection continues today. Many German families have recently purchased homes along this coast for use as summer homes, which they fly to annually, thanks to cheap and convenient air connections and a strong German currency.

Before leaving the town, plan to stroll around and look at some of the town's lovely architecture, some of which dates back to its founding just four years after Halifax.

Of all the buildings, by far the most imposing structure is **Lunenburg Academy,** built in 1894–95 high atop Gallows Hill, where it can be seen for many miles around. This is the province's only surviving academy building dating from the last century. It is full of all sorts of Victorian bits of fancy: oval-shaped portholes, towers, decorative shingles, and intricate bracketry. And when you reach the hill where this Municipal, Provincial, and Federal Heritage Building stands, you are presented with a panoramic view of the town's many beautiful old homes.

Traveling south from Lunenburg, take a fifteen-minute detour off Highway 3 and travel on Route 332 in the direction of East LaHave. Just before you reach this point you will come to the head of Rose Bay and a small sign indicating the exit to ◆ **The Ovens.** This is a sight you must not miss, for here was the scene of a major gold strike in 1861.

It still holds some gold deposits to this day. For an admission fee of $3.00, you can enter the park and pan for gold along the beach. On the day that I visited, I spoke with some men who went at least once a week, always coming away with some nuggets. It's easy to get on-the-spot prospecting lessons, as the beach is the regular haunt of helpful amateur prospectors. The management also gives periodic demonstrations of proper technique.

At The Ovens you can descend a series of concrete steps set into the side of sea caves. These are so massive that they were legend to the Micmac, who believed that a brave once traveled between this cave and a similar one on the Bay of Fundy, on the other side of Nova Scotia. Once you get to the bottom of the steps of some of the bigger caves, you will be treated to the earth-shattering boom of the waves as they crash explosively against the rocks. You can also take a boat with a guide, who will lead you right into the biggest caves.

The Ovens has campsites and some log cabins for rent, a pool, and a restaurant with a surprisingly good menu, considering its secluded location. Rates are standard to moderate. For reservations call (902) 766–4621.

After visiting The Ovens, take Highway 332 back to Route 3 outside Lunenburg and then turn south at Exit 12, onto Provincial Highway 103. After a half hour's drive, you will come to **Liverpool,** favorite haunt of the privateers.

From 1750 until the War of 1812 was resolved, Nova Scotia's and, in particular, Liverpool's ships were commissioned to roam the high seas in search of prey. Liverpudlian Enos Collins, the owner of a privateer ship called *The Packet,* was rumored to be Canada's richest man; he died with a fortune of $10 million.

The wealth brought in is evidenced by the historic buildings and museums here, recalling the wild days of the town's youth. Liverpool is the site of the oldest house in the entire collection of Nova Scotia museums, of which there are now twenty-four. To find it, exit Provincial Highway 103 on Main Street and proceed in the direction of Moose Harbour. Just after Bristol Avenue you'll see the museum at 105 Main Street, set far back on a lawn that it shares with the county museum.

Called the ✦ **Perkins House,** after its original owner, this one-and-a-half-story building was the home of a Connecticut widower who came to Nova Scotia in 1762, at age twenty-seven. Here he successfully established himself as, among other things, a justice of the court of common pleas, a judge of probate, and a member of the legislative assembly.

In this simple home, Perkins entertained privateer captains, governors, and traveling men of the cloth. He wrote about his life

Perkins House, Liverpool

in a diary that he kept faithfully from 1766 until his death in 1812. It now serves as valuable historical data on the early life of this province's settlers. A copy is on site for your perusal, and every day museum staff turn to that date's corresponding entry in his diary so that visitors can take in the history of the area's early settlers.

The entries tell of both mundane and profound concerns, from outbreaks of smallpox, to raids by American privateers, to the stuff that made up his day-to-day life with his first and second wives and their six daughters and two sons. Admission to Perkins House is free. It is open from 9:30 A.M. until 5:30 P.M. Monday through Saturday and from 1:00 to 5:00 P.M. on Sunday.

Liverpool wasn't the most tranquil place to raise children. In 1783 Americans landed at nearby Fort Point and overran the town. Through the efforts of Simeon Perkins, they were repulsed.

In the 1930s, when the museum was being established, the problem arose of how to furnish the home in period furnishings that matched the inventory of its original occupant. Pieces had to be purchased at an auction in Massachusetts.

All parts of the diary that were written in Nova Scotia have been published by the Champlain Society. The original is on display at the ◆ **Queens County Museum,** which is adjacent to Perkins House. This museum represents the warehouse of Simeon Perkins's business.

Another highlight of this museum is a diorama and model railroad, built by seniors, that demonstrate how in the 1940s the railway connected all the little communities along these shores. The shoreline has been meticulously reproduced. The attendant will set the train in motion for you, then playfully blow into a wooden whistle that makes the characteristic train sound.

If you have any ancestral roots from this end of Nova Scotia, this is a good place to trace them, since the building houses the Thomas Raddall Research Room, which features a library and genealogical records for Queens County that is operated by the historical society. Thomas Raddall was one of the province's most noteworthy writers; he published many novels set in Nova Scotia. Admission to the museum is free. It has the same hours as Perkins House next door.

Explore your artistic side at the **gallery of Roger Savage,** at 611 Mersey Point Road in a bedroom community called **Western Head.** To get there take the next right turn after Perkins House and drive down School Street, in the direction of the Western Head Lighthouse. The drive takes about 15 minutes.

Savage is one of the region's most highly esteemed artists. He not only does paintings of coastal landscapes, but also creates watercolors, portraits, and lithographs and holds workshops. He can be reached by calling (902) 354–5431.

There are a number of cozy places to stay in the area, two of which are located near wonderfully unspoiled beaches. One, **White Point Beach Lodge,** is rated 3½ stars and is quite popular. It occupies the shoreline of White Point Beach.

This well-known resort can be reached via Exit 20A or 21, off Highway 103. The restaurant here has nightly bonfires and features the local specialty: plank salmon—salmon that is barbecued over an open fire after it's been laid out on boards. There is a play area for children in the dining room, which owner

Doug Fawthrop assures me keeps the little critters out of the adults' hair quite effectively. Mussels are cooked in fire pits with hot rocks. Guests' older kids get to go on a supervised overnight camping trip to a small neighboring island, accessed by a rowboat.

You can reach the lodge by calling (800) 565–5068 from anywhere in North America, (800) 665–4863 from Nova Scotia or P.E.I. Rates are moderate.

A much smaller-scale set of beachside villas can be found at neighboring Summerville Beach, at a place called ◆ **The Quarterdeck Beachside Villas and Grill.** It provides intimate, two-story, condo-style accommodations overlooking the tranquil, spotless white sands of Summerville Beach, on a site that was occupied by much older rustic cottages for fifty years. The new villas are so close to the shoreline that you are lulled to sleep by the steady lapping of the waves.

If you are in the mood for an early morning hike, walk to the far southern end of the beach and then cross over a small arm of water via a one-time rail crossing. This leads to another tranquil little cove, where you can watch shore birds do their thing. The beach is home to piping plovers and sandpipers.

The villas have lots of pleasant little extras: propane-powered fireplace, two bathrooms, one featuring a Jacuzzi complete with rubber ducky, well-equipped kitchen facilities, a patio overlooking the ocean, and a second-floor deck, also facing the sea. The walls are decorated with original artwork, all for sale.

The restaurant here overlooks the ocean and serves plank salmon, among other delicious fare. The Quarterdeck is off Highway 103; turn at Exit 20 and head for Summerville Beach. For information and reservations–phone or fax (902) 683–2998. Rates are deluxe.

From Liverpool you have the option of turning inland onto Route 8 to experience the wilderness of **Kejimkujik National Park,** or you can continue heading south on either Route 3 or Provincial Highway 103 (which briefly overlaps Route 3) around the tip of Nova Scotia, and reserve Kejimkujik for later. For details on Keji, see pages 124–26. In the next section we will continue to follow the route southward, toward **Yarmouth,** the southern gateway to the province.

THE WESTERN LIGHTHOUSE ROUTE

Just past the town of Liverpool, on Highway 103, is a wonderful but little-known wilderness area. It is the nesting ground of endangered species and a completely unspoiled stretch of shoreline completely lacking in "development." During the piping plover's mating season, parts of this area are closed to the public.

In 1985 the province handed over 5,400 acres (2,160 hectares) of this land to the National Park Service, which now administers it as part of Kejimkujik National Park. Called the ✦ **Seaside Adjunct,** it offers two pristine beaches, both 2 miles (3 km) long, completely unspoiled wilderness and rocky headlands. (There are no facilities for human visitors, so plan accordingly.) It is very easy to miss the road for the Seaside Adjunct, so as you drive south down the one and only stretch of highway (Route 3/Provincial Highway 103), be on the lookout for a sign indicating SOUTH WEST PORT MOUTON. Take a left here.

The Seaside Adjunct is a nesting ground of the ill-fated piping plover, which has become increasingly rare due to its unfortunate habit of laying eggs in piles of rock near the shoreline. The spotted eggs look decidedly like rocks, which would be a nice form of camouflage if only they didn't get stepped on by human passersby.

Bear that in mind if you decide to walk along the pristine beaches of this coast: What may look like a rock may actually be the embryo of an endangered baby bird. So crucial is this area to the survival of piping plovers that parts of the annex are closed from late April to late July so that the birds can hatch safely.

Along with birds, you may get a look at some coastal seals as they frolic in the waves off this blissfully solitary shore.

Just south of the Seaside Adjunct, off Highway 103 and about 25 miles (40 km) from Liverpool, you will come to the ✦ **Port l'Hebert Pocket Wilderness,** a piece of woodland set aside by a pulp and paper company that has extensive land holdings in western Nova Scotia. Look for a sign on the road 6 miles (10 km) after Port Joli and just before you reach the Shelburne County line.

At Port l'Herbert you will find about 2 miles (3 km) of gravelled walking trails that cut through 150 acres (60 hectares) of woodlands and saltmarshes. These paths stretch from the small parking lot on the side of the highway, where you turned off, to the

93

shores of a tiny bay called Port L'Hebert Harbour, which draws its name from an apothecary who sailed with Samuel de Champlain in 1604. Louis l'Hebert's name lives on at Louis Head as well.

These lands are the wintering grounds of a flock of Canadian geese. They need eel grass, open water, and as little disturbance as possible to get through the winter; few places suit them as well as this site. Due to its importance, the Canadian Wildlife Service has designated the marshy shoreline a waterfowl sanctuary.

You may also spot the common yellowthroat and red-eyed vireo here. The trail is quite an easy walk, with some boardwalk aiding your travel, but if you stray far from the path you may discover your feet sinking into the bog. The water looks quite uninviting here, stained as it is a murky tea-brown. In fact, however, it is nutrient-rich, and the saltmarshes that border this bay are nurseries for all manner of sea life. Before the white man arrived, inland Micmac families came here to gather shellfish and to fish.

Once you have finished stretching your legs, return to your vehicle at the end of the trail loop and head, camera-ready, 12 miles (20 km) south on Route 3 to the scenic village of **Lockeport.** This is the site of the province's first officially designated Heritage streetscape, which slates it for historic preservation. **Crescent Beach,** which runs along the entrance to the town, was once on the back of the Canadian $50 bill.

A new visitor's information bureau overlooks the beach. Here you can change into a bathing suit or arrange the rental of a nearby cottage. Be sure to check out the tile mural by local artist Rebecca Tudor, whose studio is in Sable River. (Her work also appears on the floor of the Shelburne Visitor's Centre, described below.) Natural elements such as tulips, wildflowers, and fish blend in her pieces to create a harmony reminiscent of Tiffany's elegant stained-glass windows.

The road to Lockeport runs the length of the beach, giving the impression that you are driving along a sandbar to an island. Its location off the main highway adds to the impression that you are visiting an island unto itself. The beach is spectacular—hence its appearance on the $50 bill.

Apart from strolling around the tiny village taking pictures, there is not a lot to do here. When your interest is sated, get back in your car and head farther south on Route 3 to a string of villages peopled by the descendants of Loyalists from Nantucket and Cape Cod who came to this area after 1760.

From Lockeport it is only a half-hour's drive to **Shelburne** along Provincial Trunk Highway 3 until you reach Exit 25. Following the road will lead you into the town's historic waterfront Dock Street.

Try to park near the Visitor's Centre, which is built right at the water's edge. If you stop in, be sure to take a good look at the floor tile mosaic by Rebecca Tudor. From here all of the historic area is to your left as you face the water.

In Shelburne you can visit the ❖ **Ross-Thomson House,** a remnant from the era of the United Empire Loyalists. It is located on Charlotte Lane, which intersects Dock Street, quite near the harbor. As you walk inside the door, the most striking thing is the rich patina of the building. Goods from the era of the former store are laid out as if the company were still in business, right down to birch brooms and wooden toys.

In early 1783 the shores around here were the landing site of some 5,000 settlers from New York and the Middle Colonies of America. Acting on the promise of free land, tools, and provisions, many had chosen to leave the new republic and head north to live under British rule. This first wave of settlers was followed by another wave in the fall, many of them entrepreneurs.

By the following year the population of Shelburne was double that of Halifax, and larger than Montreal or Quebec at the time. In fact, at its peak it was the third-largest town in North America. Because of the huge influx of colonists, it has become one of the continent's genealogical treasures.

The Ross-Thomson House is the last original store building from that era. It was the site of intense trading. The owners, a pair of brothers originally from Scotland, sold local wood; fish and salt from Turk's Island; tobacco, rum, sugar, and molasses from the West Indies; fine goods from Britain; Portuguese wine, and many other local and imported items.

Little by little, however, the town's population began to dwindle. The lack of arable land meant that when the government withdrew from distributing food, living here became increasingly more difficult. By the 1820s the town had shrunk to a mere 300 souls.

The building is typical of the type favored by the Loyalists. The house shows a strong New England influence, with its gambrel roof and gables. Finished with heavy plank doors, added security came in the form of studs, bars, and a double lock. For a time the house served as the town post office; the shutter on the north window has a slot into which late mail could be posted.

Much of Shelburne's Loyalist past is still in evidence in the town, as shown by the number of buildings still standing that date from the time of the American War of Independence. Among these, one has been turned into a small inn, overlooking the harbor. Called **Cooper's Inn,** it dates from 1785 and has been sufficiently preserved and restored that it has received an award from Heritage Trust Nova Scotia. Like all of the other buildings on Dock Street, it is finished in deep-brown shingles. Located near Ross-Thomson House, this building was constructed under the direction of a blind Loyalist merchant named George Gracie.

Through the centuries it has housed mariners, shipbuilders, gentlemen esquires, merchants, and coopers. Apart from the cozy colonial atmosphere, the highlight of this place is the dining room, which features superb meals during the season, which runs from April to October. For reservations call (902) 875–4656. Rates are standard, with breakfast included.

Cooper's Inn, along with several other places on Dock Street, was part of extensive restorations undertaken prior to a visit by the newly married Prince and Princess of Wales in 1983 B.C. (Before Camilla).

Because of the facelift (the town's, not Camilla's), the harbor area is quite a pleasant place to roam aimlessly about soaking up atmosphere. Think of it as time travel. It is sufficiently authentic that it was used as the set for the 1995 movie *The Scarlet Letter*.

You will no doubt wonder how the asphalt was hidden from the camera during the filming. The solution was to truck in loads of dirt and cover the paving. No detail was too small to ignore during the making of the movie. In order to ensure that the white houses of a distant point were not evident, for example, the set designers had bushes strategically planted to obscure the distant shore.

More information on the Loyalist era can be had at another Dock Street locale, the ◆ **Shelburne County Museum.** For those of you who have families dating back to Revolutionary days and a link to Loyalists who settled in Nova Scotia, this is the place to track down some family history. The museum has extensive genealogical records. There are even eighteenth- to twentieth-century newspapers on microfilm so that you can peruse the old news at your leisure. The museum is open year-round, with summer hours Monday to Saturday from 9:30 A.M. to 5:30 P.M. From November 1 to mid-May, it closes a half hour earlier and closes for lunch from noon to 2:00 P.M. Admission is free.

Another source for genealogical information is next door to the museum, at the Shelburne County Genealogical Research Centre. Eleanor Smith is a certified genealogist on staff who assists people in tracing their Nova Scotian roots. Members of the Shelburne County Genealogical Society can search records for free, but a mere $3.00 fee gives you access to considerable research.

The center has indexed church records and vital statistics, an in-depth census, and the international genealogical index as well as records for the whole county. It also keeps newspaper statistics on various people and information on Heritage homes in the area. Smith points out that not all the families in this area were Loyalists: A number of Welsh people settled here as well as Icelandic and Scottish people. Blacks from the United States also settled in nearby Birchtown at the time of the Revolution.

Of those settlers who were Loyalist, some returned to the United States after a few years, leaving some relatives behind here. Other Shelburne-area people moved to American cities in the early 1900s. Their descendants now often come in search of distant relatives still living in this area.

Of particular interest is the history of **Birchtown,** named for General John Birch, the New York commander who gave protection to Loyalist blacks, whose direct descendants still live here. At the time of the Revolution, many black American slaves chose to take sides with the British, who promised them their freedom. Expecting equal treatment with other Loyalists, they came to live under British rule. But few of them received the land that the white Loyalists received as a matter of course, and those who did get land received substandard lots.

Most ended up working as wage laborers, but the pay was so low that a group of disbanded soldiers rioted against the unfair competition that the blacks' low wages created. The result was that twenty black Loyalist homes were destroyed in ten days of rioting.

In 1783, when the village was settled by 1,000 freed slaves, it was the largest free black settlement in North America. But by 1792 the settlers in Birchtown were fed up, and they joined other black Loyalists in the province who had decided that a return to Africa was in order. That year 1,200 of them left the colony and founded Freetown in Sierra Leone.

Recent archaeological digs in the neighborhood of Birchtown have revealed remnants of these settlers' early days. Eleanor Smith points out that some of them had homes that were little more than holes dug in the ground and then covered with a roof.

One other Dock Street site is worth a special mention: ◆ **The Dory Shop.** You may already have visited a dory shop along the "Lighthouse Route" (Route 3), but if you haven't already done so, this one is operated by the Nova Scotia museum system and comprises three stories of dory making memorabilia. A factory from 1880 to 1970, it is all that is left in the town of its original seven dory shops. It opened as a museum in 1983 and featured as its star attraction master dory builder Sidney Mahaney, who made dories according to the traditional methods he learned in his youth. Mahaney began making dories at age seventeen and continued until his death at age ninety-six in 1993. One of his miniature dories was given to Prince William as a present.

A large photograph of Mahaney, decked out in a Nova Scotia tartan shirt, acts as a backdrop for his last hand-built dory, which is displayed here. Back in the early days, this particular shop produced two dories a day, and sold them for $18 apiece. When Mahaney started, in 1914, his wages were 45 cents a day. (They reached their peak back then at $2.00 a day, after a man had received a raise every three years.)

Anyone who has lived along Canada's Atlantic coast has at one time or another placed personal safety in the hands of one of these reliable little boats. The story of their construction and the role they have played in inshore fishery is fascinating.

On the premises you will find an information booth that can fill you in on local events. Admission to the Dory Shop is free, but donations are welcome. Hours of operation from mid-June to mid-September are 9:30 A.M. to 5:30 P.M. daily. Phone the Dory Shop at (902) 875–3219.

After you've visited the town of Shelburne, you can resume your drive down the Lighthouse Route, (Highway 3) or Provincial Highway

103 until twenty minutes later, when the roads converge at the head of Barrington Bay in a village called Barrington Passage.

If you ever had the urge to get onto a Cape Islander boat, here is your chance. The Barrington Passage tourist bureau has one you can visit. (It's also on Highway 3.) The Seal Island Lighthouse Museum here is open to the public, and you can climb the five stories to the top, which offers a panoramic view of the bay.

Continue along Highway 3 in Barrington until you cross the Barrington River, indicated by a road sign. Here you'll find the ◆ **Barrington Woolen Mill,** where you can get a good look at an old-time water turbine–powered woolen mill. This had its beginnings in 1882 as a community enterprise, to provide fishermen with wool clothing. Inside the mill is a magnificent wall hanging that was woven by Bessie Murray. In addition to its depiction of Nova Scotia's history, the wall hanging features a piper wearing the Nova Scotia tartan, which was designed by Murray. Outside is a pleasant picture: The mill overlooks a rushing stream and is quite lovely.

For several decades the mill was an important supplier of specialized woolen goods for the people of this region. It is now part of the Nova Scotia Museum system and features jennies, looms, a dye house, and equipment for scouring wool. It is open from June 15 to September 30 from 9:30 A.M. to 5:30 P.M. Monday to Saturday, and Sunday from 1:00 to 5:30 P.M. Phone them at (902) 657–2185.

A change of pace from the old dory shops and elegant old homes is the ◆ **Old Meeting House in Barrington,** located at the head of Barrington Bay. The barnlike meetinghouse was built in 1765 by Loyalist pilgrims who used it as a place of worship and for public meetings. It is the oldest New England–style meetinghouse in the province. Barrington Township itself was founded in 1761 by fifty families of Cape Cod planters, who brought their religion, customs, and building style north with them.

To meet the religious needs of all denominations, they built the meetinghouse for ". . . all preachers of the Gospel . . ." Eventually, the different denominations built their own places of worship. The old meetinghouse almost fell prey to the wrecking ball until a community group saved it. It is now part of the Nova Scotia Museum system.

Be sure to stroll through the graveyard adjacent to the building, where you will see the markers of many of the area's early settlers. One fine day, in the middle of a funeral on the morning of May 4, 1783, the mourners glanced away at a great cloud of white sails crowding the harbor mouth. There they saw the singular event that was to transform Shelburne into one of the most important towns on the continent. That morning a convoy of transports carried into the harbor thousands of United Empire Loyalists, newly exiled from their New England homes.

The meetinghouse is open from June 15 to September 30 from 9:30 A.M. to 5:30 P.M. Monday to Saturday, and Sundays from 1:00 to 5:30 P.M.

You can live in Nova Scotia for decades and never visit the remote fishing villages of the southernmost tip of the province unless you are headed for one of the ferries to Portland or Bar Harbor, Maine. As such, this is decidedly off-trail and well worth some lazy puttering.

As for archetypical fishing villages, they don't get more authentic than ◆ **Clark's Harbour, Cape Sable Island,** the southernmost part of Nova Scotia. Once the British won their final battle with the French, this whole area opened up for settlement, in large part encouraged by the Expulsion of the Acadians and supplemented by the American Revolution, which followed a few years later.

One of the first places to be newly settled by people from the other colonies was Cape Sable Island. In 1761 the island was settled by forty families from outer Cape Cod. The following year a number of whalers and their families from Nantucket moved into neighboring areas. Even Halifax harbor's eastern waterfront was a site of a Cape Cod whaler settlement, as evidenced by some of the houses near the Old Dartmouth waterfront.

In Cape Sable Island especially, traces of the Cape Cod housing style and even the accents linger. Fishing and related industries have always been its mainstay. It was here in 1907 that the Cape Island boat was first built for fishing off the coast. To this day it is the standard for small fishing boats that can withstand the cruel seas of the North Atlantic.

They are not as elegant as the schooners of yore, but the Cape Islander, like the dory, is outstandingly seaworthy, sitting high in the water. The standard Cape is 38 feet (11 m) long, with a

12-foot (3.6-m) beam. The old ones had a pulpit on the bow for harpooning.

Stay on Highway 3 as you proceed around the southern tip of the province and you will see a string of small fishing and farming communities peopled by the descendants of Loyalist planters and returned Acadians, among others: **Ste.-Anne du Ruisseau** and **West, Middle West,** and **Lower West Pubnico** are a few of these villages, partially peopled by the descendants of the Acadians who originally settled here in 1653. If you look carefully, you will see traces of these early days, from an old stone bridge to the ✦**Musée Acadien** in West Pubnico.

This Acadian Museum is a homestead dating back to 1864. Today it contains artifacts from Acadian pioneer days along with land grant documents from the 1700s. To visit the place turn off Highway 3 onto Highway 335 and drive east for 3 miles (5 km) until you reach West Pubnico. Admission is free. It is open daily from 9:00 A.M. until 5:00 P.M. from June 1 until the end of August.

After you check out the local history, hop into your car and drive to the end of the line, about 2.5 miles (4 km), to Charlesville. There is nothing much going on here, though the shoreline was the landing site of well over one hundred Sikh refugees a few years back. Stop anywhere to buy a bottle of soda pop. Naively ask, "Say, wasn't this where all those guys landed?" and you'll be treated to the full story. It's a great icebreaker.

The name Pubnico is derived from the Micmac word for "cleared land." The actual village of Pubnico (not Middle, West or Lower West) was settled by transplanted New Englanders who came in 1761, filling the void created by the expulsion of Acadians from the region.

Just before you reach Yarmouth proper, turn off Highway 3 at Arcadia and follow the sign for Kelly Cove and Chebogue Point. Soon after joining the lupin-edged shore road, you will come to the tiny **Town Point Cemetery** in **Chebogue.**

Apart from the many old settlers who found their final resting place here, a sad and beautiful love story is linked to the place. Among the weathered headstones you will find a life-size carving of a woman reclining, as if asleep, on sheaves of wheat, sickle in hand. This is the grave of one Margaret Webster, who died in 1861. Several years before this date, her Yarmouth-born husband was a young medical student in Scotland.

One day, he was walking through the fields when he came upon just such a sleeping figure. He paused for a long time to watch the beautiful woman, exhausted by her work, catching forty winks. When the woman awoke, he introduced himself, and soon a relationship developed. The two were married, and that would have been the end of the story had Margaret Webster not died suddenly.

The bereaved young man returned to Yarmouth, where he searched until he found a talented artist to make a marble effigy of his lady, who reclines to this day, seemingly asleep, on the sheaves of wheat where her husband first fell in love with her.

It's just a statue and a sentimental side trip, but the detour is worthwhile. The road is strewn with lupin, and if you look out over the water, you will get a sweeping view of the Tusket Islands.

Westbound from Yarmouth, the Lighthouse Route takes on a new name, the Evangeline Trail, in honor of Longfellow's epic poem about the banished Acadians. Therefore, you will enter Yarmouth on the very last leg of the Lighthouse Route and meet the beginning of the Evangeline Trail where Highway 1 meets Highway 3.

The junction is also the corner of Starr's Road and Main Street, down by the waterfront in beautiful downtown Yarmouth, population 7,781. From this corner take a left, continue half a block, and keep your eyes open for the ❖ **Firefighter's Museum** on your left at 451 Main Street.

If you are arriving from Maine on a ferry, you'll be departing the boat just slightly farther down that same waterfront road. In this case, as you drive off the Marine Atlantic Ferry, turn left onto Main Street. Continue past the Parade Street intersection to 431 Main Street on your right. The Firefighter's Museum is the only provincial firefighter's museum in Canada. They have every type of fire engine ever in use in Nova Scotia as well as all kinds of other vintage firefighting gear.

There is an 1880 Silsby Steamer that looks like a madman's boiler on wheels. A bright-red hand pumper dates back to 1819; it is so dinky that one expects a monkey and organ grinder to be next to it and a hot roasted-chestnut concession to be operating out of it. The shiny metal doodad-covered Holloway Chemical Engine from 1892 is so ornate that it could donate parts for Cinderella's carriage. Apart from the three horse-drawn steamers, the museum has some antique toy fire engines and other nostalgia for anybody who ever wanted to grow up to be a firefighter.

Firemen swear this is the best collection they've ever seen anywhere. The **National Exhibit Centre,** in the same complex, features traveling exhibits. For more information write to 431 Main Street, Yarmouth, N.S. B5A 1G9, or call (902) 742–5525. Open year-round, admission is $1.00 per person, $2.00 per family. Hours are 9:00 A.M. to 5:00 P.M. Monday to Saturday in July and August. The rest of the year they open from 10:00 A.M. to 4:00 P.M. Monday to Friday, but close daily from noon until 2:00 P.M.

Before leaving Yarmouth, you may want to explore local history at the ◆ **Yarmouth County Museum,** 22 Collins Street. Among other artifacts here, you will find a 400-pound (182-kg) stone inscribed by a group of Vikings including, it is believed, Leif Ericson, in the year A.D. 1007. The inscription is nothing outstanding, being a Norseman's version of "Kilroy was here," but it is offered as proof that Christopher Columbus was not the first European to reach the New World and that Jacques Cartier and John Cabot were mere Johnny-come-latelys as well. The runic symbols are drawn from one of approximately a dozen distinct Norse alphabets, so the translation, although doubtful, is roughly believed to read: "Leif to Eric raises this monument."

The museum is a great place for would-be sailors, Viking or otherwise. The collection of Age of Sail artifacts, including ship portraits and models, is drawn from a seafaring past that saw Yarmouth as the home of the third-largest merchant navy in the world. When sailing ships ruled the day, this little town boasted the world's highest per capita ship tonnage. The remnants of this legacy are found at this museum, including one of the largest collections of marine paintings in the country as well as a lighthouse lens, a stagecoach, historic costumes, furniture, tools, and glass. For more information call (902) 742–5539.

To get to the Yarmouth County Museum from the Firefighter's Museum, turn left when you exit the building and go south down Main Street, in the direction of the ferry terminal, until you get to the Collins Street intersection. Turn left again and you will be at the door of the museum. Admission is $1.00 for adults; students are half fare; children under fourteen get in for 25 cents.

After leaving the museum, get back onto Main Street and continue past Starrs Road. Turn left on Vancouver Street, then take a left again onto Route 304. Follow this route to **Overton** and **Cape Fourchu.** In a matter of minutes after leaving the town of Yarmouth, you'll be deep in the heart of photographer's heaven: Cape Fourchu is one of the most photogenic lighthouses in the province, set at the tip of rugged granite coastline. (At one point a high wall en route to Cape Fourchu protects cars from the waves on rough days, and the road seems precariously close to the water.) The original lighthouse, built in 1840, was replaced by a more up-to-date facility in the 1960s.

Just past the lighthouse is the **Leif Erikson Picnic Park,** the landing site of the famous Viking explorer. Apart from its historical significance, the park overlooks spectacular coastline and offers visitors a good spot to picnic, tables and all.

After this stop head back to town until you reach the end of the little peninsula.

This is the end of the Lighthouse Route and the Atlantic coastline. From here the communities change from descendants of the Germans and Loyalists, whalers and privateers, to communities with a strong Acadian heritage. To explore this next region turn right onto Route 1.

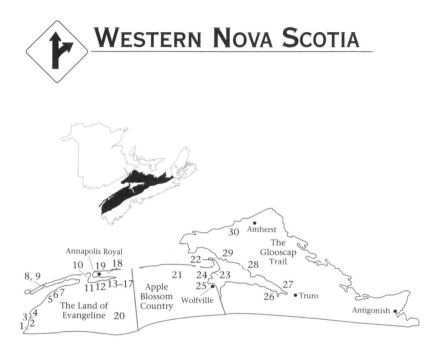

WESTERN NOVA SCOTIA

1. World's smallest wooden lift bridge
2. Churchill Mansion
3. Duck Pond Inn/Space Barn
4. Mavilette Beach
5. Gross Coques/gastropod hunting/artist Claude Chaloux
6. Couquillages & Couleurs/ Galerie Boutique
7. L'Eglise St.-Bernard
8. Digby Neck
9. Balancing Rock
10. Pines Resort Hotel
11. The Mountain Gap Inn
12. Upper Clements Park
13. Annapolis Royal
14. Old Post Office
15. Newman's
16. Fort Anne
17. Annapolis Royal Historic Gardens
18. Habitation
19. Delap's Cove
20. Kejimkujik National Park
21. Oaklawn Farm Zoo
22. Cape Split
23. Planter's Barracks Country Inn
24. Prescott House
25. Apple Blossom Festival
26. Rafting on the tidal wave
27. Joy Laking Gallery
28. Five Islands Provincial Park
29. Fundy Geological Museum
30. Joggins Fossil Centre

WESTERN NOVA SCOTIA

Along the Nova Scotian shoreline of the Bay of Fundy is a culture that has withstood massive deportation and centuries of isolation. As visitors ramble along Route 1, the little communities of this Acadian heartland stretch one into the other, giving the impression of a massive, church-dotted "Main Street" that extends right through the villages where the French first set up shop in their Canadian adventure.

This region boasts the first ever European settlement on Canadian soil. It was from here that the governments of France and, later, England ruled the whole region of Acadia, which included Nova Scotia and New Brunswick.

Possession of the area fluctuated between the English and French armies. In the end, when France lost control for good, the settlers' neutrality came into question. Finally the new military commanders made a decision that was to echo as far south as Louisiana.

THE LAND OF EVANGELINE

It was from the shores of Northwestern Nova Scotia that thousands of Acadians were forced to board ships that would disperse them along the eastern seaboard and as far south as Louisiana, where they eventually became known as Cajuns. Among the exiles dispersed was a couple separated on their wedding day. Years later the bride, who had become a nun, finally found her husband— on his deathbed. This was the true story that inspired the epic poem *Evangeline,* for which this region is now named.

The Acadians, once exiled from Nova Scotia and now returned, can boast of a thriving Francophone culture and lively community life.

The Evangeline Trail, which is actually Route 1, begins in Yarmouth (end point of the Lighthouse Route), at the intersection of Main and Vancouver Streets.

Traveling east along this historic route, you will shortly come to **Sandford,** a scenic harbor and home of what is claimed to be the ❦ **world's smallest wooden lift bridge.** To see this bridge, turn left at the Sandford Breakwater and drive right down to the wharf. The wharf is strewn with mountains of seashells, photographs of which look like abstract art. From here you will

World's Smallest Wooden Lift Bridge

see what initially appears to be an upside down V. That is the bridge. A winch operates it, with the help of whoever is standing by, but the bridge is never flat, so small boats can pass under easily. Walking up it is like crossing a steep ramp.

Just after this wonder of engineering, you will come to Darling Lake and, high up on a hill just off the coastal highway, the one-time home of a hero and industrialist who is reputed to still haunt the place. ◆ **Churchill Mansion** is now an inn, after six decades during which its sole occupants were a pair of ghosts, according to owner and innkeeper Bob Benson. Many of its original light fixtures, furnishings, and features remain intact, since a caretaker maintained the place for many years after Aaron Churchill's passing in 1920. (For thirty-three of those years, there was $3 million worth of jewelry locked up in a safe that no one bothered opening.)

The Churchill Mansion is host to a **Psychic Fair** every May, "During the full moon," Benson intones gleefully. The rest of the year, there are visits from fans of the paranormal, some of whom swear they have been visited by Churchill, the original owner of the mansion. The innkeeper refers to him as Aaron, in tones that imply an old acquaintance.

Aaron Churchill became famous in 1866 as a sixteen-year-old crewman aboard an ocean-bound ship off the coast of Labrador. When the ship's rudder broke, Aaron went over the side six times attempting to fix the damage. In frigid water temperatures and life-threatening conditions, the young man persevered. His eventual success saved the ship's crew and cargo, and saw him rewarded with a check for $1,500 from Lloyd's of London.

Churchill was descended from the same line as Britain's wartime prime minister. If a streak of greatness ran through the Churchills, so also did the supernatural. Bob Benson has been in contact with owners of other "Churchill mansions" built by close relatives of Aaron Churchill. Several of them have reputations as haunted houses. One of them, in Savannah, Georgia, is the starting point for a walking tour of haunted houses.

After Churchill died, it became the home of his "niece" Lottie (perhaps his daughter, resulting from a liason between Churchill and his brother's wife), who had been put away in an asylum for many years following the mysterious death of her illegitimate infant. (A staff of thirteen servants saw to her every need while she did "soft time.") Following her death she was buried alongside Churchill in the neighboring cemetery, where she remains to this day except for the occasional late-night sightings of her wandering apparition.

There are eight guest rooms in the inn, which is open from May 1 to mid-November. For reservations call (902) 649–2818. Rates are standard.

Twenty minutes outside of Yarmouth, and continuing along the west coast up the Bay of Fundy on Route 1, you'll come to **Beaver River,** on the Yarmouth/Digby county line. Turn right just at the county line and drive past a few houses until you see the sign for the ◆ **Duck Pond Inn.** Here you will find a former NASA scientist who has created the ◆ **"Space Barn Museum"** and is running a bed and breakfast. These accommodations are ideal for recovering from the ferry trip or waiting for the next day's boat. Harry Tailor offers guests big four-poster beds and hearty gourmet breakfasts.

Tailor, who still works as a consultant with NASA, gives the Space Barn tour in costume. He calls it, "A learning experience, not just a gee whiz type of thing." The two-hour tour includes an introductory twenty-minute video, complete with clips of launches. Exhibits include instruments from space flights, a heat-resistant tile from a space shuttle, and even a plaster cast of the hand of one of the astronauts who traveled to the moon. Admission is $4.00 for adults and $3.00 for children. Guests at the Duck Pond Inn get the tour for free. Plan to book ahead with a few friends, as Tailor prefers to put on his production only for groups of several people. Try to work in a space barn tour as part of an overnight stay. Apart from the rare exhibits and the slide show in the barn, you can soak in the atmosphere of the elegant inn, which is a provincially designated Heritage property and the one-time home of a sea captain.

The setting is only a stone's throw from the beach. Nearly one hundred species of local shells can be found in these waters; examples of the shells are on display at the Yarmouth County Museum. For information on the inn or the Space Barn Museum, call (902) 649–2249. Rates are standard.

Along Highway 1 from Beaver River you'll drift into Salmon River and then the gorgeous ❖ **Mavilette Beach,** which winds for about 1 mile (1.6 km) along the shoreline to Cape St. Mary's.

This is undoubtedly one of the prettiest beaches in this end of the country, although the water temperature is low enough to chill champagne. There is a provincial picnic park and walking trails along the grassy dunes.

Boardwalks protect the sea grasses, which are all that holds the sand back from the relentless forces of Mother Nature. Stay on the boardwalks and heed the signs at this beach—the day I visited there was a sudden drop of 10 feet (3 m) or so at the end of the boardwalk, marked only by a tiny sign and barrier.

Beachcombing on the fine white sand can yield a wide choice of shells and driftwood. Be aware that the extensive sand flats of low tide are a temporary thing; here you will be reminded that the Bay of Fundy has the highest tides in the world. What people often don't realize is how fast the water level can change. But as the water rises, the sand heats it up to a less brutal temperature for swimming.

There is excellent seafood at the **Cape View Diner,** in particular whole fresh lobster and Acadian specialties. Alongside are the Cape View Motel and cottages. For reservations call (902) 645–2258, or write to P.O. Box 9, Salmon River, Digby County, N.S. B0W 2Y0.

Farther along on the route is **Smuggler's Cove,** a rocky stretch of shoreline with massive sea caves that are well known in the area because of its historic link to smuggling and rumrunning. The contraband was hidden in the "caves" that the waves carved out of the rock and that are hidden during high tide.

I visited this place years ago and had to climb down the cliffs with ropes. Now you can go down a set of steps, and the headland above the cove has been made into a provincial picnic park.

These days smugglers have been replaced by people in sea kayaks entering the cave. Indian legend says that a brave once traveled between the largest of these sea caves and one at the Ovens in Lunenburg county; most kayakers don't go in much farther than the rumrunners did.

In **Church Point** (by its French name, **Pointe de l'Eglise**), a short way up the road, is **Université Ste.-Anne,** which is the province's French-language university. Especially because of the university's existence, this is a culturally rich area. The school acts as a magnet for Acadian artisans in Nova Scotia. The university archives also offer visitors with Acadian French ancestors a chance to trace their roots.

The campus lines the shore and is stretched out alongside the road. Just beyond it is **Église Ste.-Marie,** or **Church of St. Mary's,** the tallest wooden church in North America, which you can see from far off. This church was actually designed in France. The 185-foot (56-m) steeple had to be secured against hurricane-force winds with 40 tons (36 metric tons) of stone ballast. To make "stone" pillars to support the roof, the builders used tree trunks covered over with plaster. The "marble" arches are wooden also. Small booklets covering the history of the village and its church are sold here, and a bilingual guide is available for tours. The door of the church is always open in the daytime; no phone number is given.

For something unusual to put on your roof, visit the studio of Joe Bengivenni, a blacksmith, who makes weather vanes and other artful objects in his studio. He operates here year-round;

during the off-season you can visit by appointment. To get to his studio, turn off the shore road in Church Point and get onto Rural Route 1. The studio is on the Lower Mill Road in **Concession,** 6 miles (10 km) inland from Church Point. Bengivenni's phone number is (902) 769–2516.

If you continue along Highway 1 after Church Point, you will come to ✿ **Grosses Coques** (translation: "Big Clams"). Keep on your toes, though, because in a flash it turns into **Belliveau Cove.**

This place is a good spot to explore shore ecology, particularly periwinkles. There are sevcral different species of periwinkles (the gastropod, not the evergreen), and they are abundant in the Bay of Fundy area because of the tides. If you go down to the shore to look for them, be sure you know when the tide is due to come in, because the beach—and your route out—might end up underwater in an astoundingly short period of time.

The water can rise more than 50 feet (15 m) in some areas of the Bay of Fundy, to the highest levels anywhere in the world. This once caused Joe Howe, Nova Scotian patriot, journalist, and eventually provincial politician to exclaim, in response to a parliamentary put-down, "How high do *your* tides rise?"

His nineteenth-century rebuke still gets a chuckle in some places these days, perhaps making it a record for old jokes. Just keep it in mind if you decide to leave your shoes on a rock somewhere and go strolling out on a large expanse of shoreline.

If you go ✿ **gastropod hunting** in Grosses Coques, you may see ✿ **artist Claude Chaloux,** who does his primitive firings at the beach. He works in stone and clay, which he paints and waxes. He creates primitive human and animal forms. Claude Chaloux's studio, Art & Mineraux (902–837–7145), is in Church Point, right on Route 1. It is open from mid-May to December, 1:00 to 6:00 P.M. His work is also displayed at several other provincial galleries: Le Motif in Chéticamp, Cape Breton, Other Art Gallery in Halifax, and the Atlantic Arts Alliances, also in Halifax.

Just before Grosses Coques ends and Belliveau Cove begins, the road crosses a small river. Immediately after this point a small sign will direct you to the old **Acadian Cemetery.** You'll drive down a road that stretches to the shore, where boardwalks offer the possibility of a walk along windswept **Major Point Beach.**

Nature lovers will love the rugged scenery at this end of the province and the opportunity to watch migratory birds, collect wildflowers, and see whales and dolphins offshore. Artists find the area inspiring, too; you'll find a number of them in this area.

A tiny, almost closetlike chapel has been erected at the site of the Acadian Cemetery. At the time of the Expulsion of the Acadians, many of them hid in the woods, aided and abetted by their Micmac allies. Some made their way to Cape Breton, which was then still in French hands. But others quietly resumed life here after a time, and their earthly remains eventually came to join those of their ancestors, the first white settlers in Canada, in the Grosses Coques cemetery. The original rough wooden crosses have been replaced by new ones, which are arranged in exactly the same way as the former markers. The handful of souls put to rest here date as far back as the 1770s.

Once you leave the cemetery and the boardwalks of Major Point Beach, you can drop in on artist Denise Comeau-Leblanc, whose ◈ **Coquillages & Couleurs/Galerie Boutique** is located in Belliveau Cove. She draws her inspirations from nature as well as from the Acadian community and culture, and works in various media. Her paintings are shown widely in the region. You can find her at 3358 Route 2, 0.2 mile (400 m) from the **Belliveau Cove Wharf.** Belliveau Cove Wharf is one of the prettiest little wharves in this part of the province, with its boats stranded at low tide and a tiny lighthouse to the left. The gallery is open daily from 10:00 A.M. to 5:00 P.M. from May to December. Call (902) 873–7116.

Following Route 1 in the direction of Halifax, you'll come next to the tiny village of St. Bernard, population 305. From far off you will see arising out of the countryside ◈ **L'Église St.-Bernard** (Church of St. Bernard), a massive granite Gothic church, built entirely by the congregation. Construction, which began in 1910, was not completed for thirty-two years. The church is enormous; it can easily accommodate a thousand people, a congregation comprised of several entire villages. Building materials were supplied by the local population, making the creation of the church a mini-industry in itself. The stone was quarried in Shelburne and then hauled by train from 120 miles away (193.5 km.)

Note that L'Église St.-Bernard is at a crossroads in the highway called Junction 28, after which Route 1 is essentially swallowed up by TransCanada Highway Route 101.

Another interesting side trip presents itself in the area of **Weymouth,** which you can reach in only a few minutes if you turn inland from Gilbert Cove, at Junction 28, and follow the old trunk highway. The provincial highway seems to be mysteriously swallowed up by the TransCanada at this junction anyway, so remember when you return to the route that you will be following the Highway 101.

In the meantime you can make the short detour to **Sissiboo Falls** to explore an area that was once a logging boomtown. Weymouth was originally called Sissiboo, a Micmac name, when it was founded by Loyalists in 1783. Compared to other Loyalist towns, settlement here was not a huge success. It was named after Weymouth, Massachusetts, after a number of people from that place settled in and things were looking up.

Over the years the town and the surrounding area became a lumbering center. In 1895 a family moved in from Alsace-Lorraine, along the French/German border. The Stehlin family included famous engineers, and one of the Stehlins operated the first steam engine in France. When they came to Weymouth, the family, which had nine sons, purchased 10,000 acres of timberland about 17 miles (27 km) inland from Weymouth in the vicinity of Sissiboo Falls.

They gave the place the ambitious name of New France, and there they established huge sawmills, cleared the land, and hired local workers until the number of residents in New France swelled to fifty. Wooden rails were built to deliver the lumber to town, using a locomotive built in Yarmouth. A passenger car was attached at the back to taxi people to town and back, and all year the private railway hauled lumber into Weymouth.

Soon a store and then a small school were built to accommodate the community. Although a large dam supplied water power to run the mills, the Stehlin family soon installed a General Electric generator, at a cost of $1,850. The tiny community was the first village in the province where electric light was used, and soon the whole place was lit up—the store, the school, and every home.

For ten years the place was a boomtown, a wonder of modern living! Then decay set in, no doubt aided and abetted by unfortunate forestry practices. All the nearest lumber had been cut, and the railway, since it was made of wood, began to rot away. There are still traces of the old settlement, some ruins of the old buildings, rotted wooden carcasses where once a private rail line hauled fresh-felled cargo. A public road will still take you as far as

Riverdale, into the land the Stehlins once proudly settled, then abandoned. Pack a lunch and putter around on your own, because you won't find any tour guides or concession stands here.

Returning to the coastal route, you'll come to **Gilbert Cove,** which has a pretty little lighthouse that has been restored. The lighthose and grounds are worth visiting, and there is a spot for picnicking here.

Around 10 miles (16 km) past Gilbert Cove on TransCanada Highway 101, you will reach Digby. From Digby follow Route 217 down a long narrow peninsula ending in a ferry ride to **Long Island,** which is followed by another short ferry ride to **Brier Island.** The whole narrow strip of land is referred to as ◆ **Digby Neck.** The ferries are timed so that if you don't stop, you can meet the second ferry without waiting. Boats run hourly twenty-four hours a day, leaving the mainland on the half hour.

Along with Digby Neck's offer of dolphins and five species of whales, the site is crisscrossed in the spring and fall by three flyways of migratory birds from the Arctic, Europe, and Canada. Birdwatchers have a chance to spot specimens of 130 species, including grebes, kittiwakes, and razorbills. The island is also home to fifteen different varieties of wild orchid and is dotted with the yellow blossoms of the mountain aven, a flower found only here and in the White Mountains of New Hampshire.

On top of all this, Digby Neck is one of the best places to get a look at the bizarre rock formations that you will no doubt see photographs of in many local tourist publications. The best place to see the rocky cliffs is a spot on Long Island marked quite inconspicuously by a hand-painted sign announcing ◆ **Balancing Rock.** It's easy to zoom past this small sign just past Tiverton as you race to meet the ferry to Brier Island. (The ferry departures are timed so that there is no waiting if you drive immediately from one boat to the next.)

If time allows, plan to skip one crossing and stop to check out the Balancing Rock. If not, be sure to stop when you are returning from Brier Island.

It really is a must-see spot. Previously, however, it was quite inaccessible. In the spring of 1995, local officials finally built a series of steps that make exploration of this bit of coastline far safer. Now the walk of a mile or so (1.6 km) is just an hour round-trip. At the end of the long series of steps built alongside the cliffs, you'll descend to a series of massive, sharply angled basalt boulders, the most spectacular of which is the "Balancing Rock," a natural Leaning Tower of Pisa–type affair. It exceeds the height of three grown men and is perched along the cliff as if at any moment it could topple.

There are only a few choices for accommodation if you want to enjoy some nature walks and explore Long Island further. In **Sandy Cove,** which is a pretty community flanked on both sides by beaches, you can stay at the **Olde Village Inn** on Route 217 west. This inn is a structure that dates back to 1890. Sandy Cove is a promising spot for rock-hounding. For reservations call (800) 834–2206.

On Brier Island you can stay at the **Brier Island Lodge,** which also has a good restaurant. You can't miss the lodge; you can actually see it from Long Island and as you approach Brier Island by boat. Its main building is a huge log structure built on a headland to the far right end of the island. The hoteliers can book whale-watching tours for you and provide maps of the island. Rooms are standard to moderate. For further information call (902) 839–2300.

Due to the depth of its tides, the waters of the Bay of Fundy have a high salt content. Consequently, they are teeming with zooplankton, which in turn attract herring and mackerel, the favorite snacking foods of whales. The result is that the tiny 3-mile (5-km) –long Brier Island is renowned for whale and dolphin watching. Sightings are guaranteed on the daily **whale-watching cruises,** with different species making their appearance at varying times of the year.

When I went on a cruise, minke whales were about, and we got quite close to them. (I also noticed that quite a few passengers looked a little green around the gills, so take something for seasickness if you are at all prone to it!)

Along with enjoying the wildflowers and the animals, you can take a long walk along the shore to see the massive, spectacular basalt rocks. Many of the best hikes are detailed on the map supplied by the Brier Island Lodge.

At Green Head, at the southwest tip of the island, you can follow a path that leads along a fascinating stretch of basalt cliffs, which also offers an excellent view of Peter's Island and its lighthouse.

From the shore you can still see the different layers of rocks, one color piled on top of another, and flocks of seabirds that make it their home. This area has been compared to the Giant's Causeway in Ireland.

Virginia Tudor, the innkeeper at Brier Island Lodge, told me that most of their visitors over the years have been naturalists, who come to study the wildlife. She points out that two thirds of the island are held by the Nature Conservancy. Another interesting fact about Brier Island is that most of the residents have relatives on Grand Manan Island. Years ago, Tudor explained, before roads came in, the people in this area got around only by boat, so the closest communities included Grand Manan, which even by today's standards would seem to be quite a drive.

There is a walk from the back door of Brier Island Lodge to **Seal Cove,** where you can watch seals in their natural habitat. The inn's two dogs lead people on this hike, which culminates at the **Grand Passage Lighthouse.** Although small, the island has three lighthouses. More than sixty shipwrecks have occurred around Brier Island. The salvage has formed part of its enduring legacy. The **Oddfellows Hall,** for example, is a fraternal lodge built completely of salvage from the 1908 shipwreck of the *Aurora.* You'll see bits and pieces of old boats all over Brier Island.

When you want to leave Digby Neck, you will be returning by the same two ferries, the *Spray* and the *Joshua Slocum,* this time for free, since you have to pay only to get on the islands, not off them. (Note that both ferries are named in honor of famous Digby-area sailor Joshua Slocum, who was the first to sail single-handedly around the world in his ship the *Spray.*)

Once off the islands, drive right off the boat onto Route 217 and continue until you get to the point where this long peninsula was connected to Nova Scotia in the first place. Take Junction 26 and turn onto Route 303, which will take you into **Digby.**

This is the docking site of the ferry from New Brunswick. The wharf in Digby also is home to the world's largest scallop fleet, hence the presence throughout the province's menus of Digby Scallops.

The area offers excellent photographic opportunities, as well as golfing. One spot favored by golfers is the ❖ **Pines Resort Hotel,** which includes a Norman-style mansion and cottages scattered about landscaped lawns. For reservations call (800) 667–4637. Rates are deluxe.

A cozy, conveniently located place to stay, with a 2½-star rating, is ❖ **The Mountain Gap Inn.** It is just a short drive farther north of Digby, in **Smith's Cove,** making it a good staging point for either a trip to Digby Neck or day trips to Annapolis and neighboring areas. To get to Smith's Cove, take either Exit 24 or 25 off Highway 101.

Mountain Gap Inn is a resort with all the amenities, including a pool and tennis court, and a calming atmosphere, with its many perennial flower gardens trimming the cabins and pathways. Nightly bonfires here are a good excuse to hang out on warm summer nights. The inn is built on a grassy headland overlooking a tidal beach, accessible by a set of wooden steps.

You may notice that in this area of Nova Scotia in particular, the fog comes in with the tide, and quite often goes out with it as well. Days can start off in a quite unpromising way, only to recover, becoming sunny after the tide recedes. It's always a good idea to have a windbreaker handy in this kind of climate.

The entire place is finished in knotty pine, including the cozy restaurant, which serves the hearty breakfasts included in the room price.

Mountain Gap Inn arranges a number of different holiday packages, in particular those built around golf and whale watching. To reserve a room or package, call (800) 565–5020. Rates are moderate.

Continue along Route 1 for a few miles after the Mountain Gap Inn to ❖ **Upper Clements Park,** which has been operating for several years now, with some changes in management and style. There used to be half-day tickets, but now you should plan on arriving early if you want to make the most of the visit. A ride pass for the day includes admission to the restaurant's buffet and costs about $15.

Upper Clements Park has, among other attractions, a rattly wooden roller-coaster that covers a large, hilly section of what was once an apple orchard. If the roller-coaster is your reason for visiting the park, be sure to ask if if it is in operation on that particular day, before you plunk down your Visa for a ride pass.

As you exit this park, you'll notice the sign for the **Upper Clements Wildlife Park** about a mile and a half (2 km) along on the same road. If you didn't stop by here before visiting the amusement park, you may want to now. Admission is free, and you can stretch your legs while you take a look at some native

Nova Scotian species like cougar, porcupines, foxes, groundhogs, deer, and moose. You may also see the Queen's royal red deer as you stroll along the walking trails.

Past Upper Clements you'll have the opportunity to visit the village of ◆ **Annapolis Royal,** which recalls the times of eastern Canada's first European settlements.

The community, which boasts the oldest thoroughfare in the country, is one of the prettiest little villages in this end of the province. It is small, but its historical significance ensures that a considerable number of people visit in the summer. The village has retained its well-mannered charm and historical character, however. There are lots of beautiful, big old homes, many of which have been turned into bed-and-breakfast establishments or inns.

A walking tour, mapped out in a brochure called "Footprints and Footnotes" is available at most of the village businesses. Following the tour at a leisurely pace should take you about an hour.

The "Footprints and Footnotes" walk begins with a monument erected on the site of a Mohawk fort built in 1712. You can see this cairn down on the waterfront, on Lower Saint George Street. At a time when the British and French were constantly wrangling for supremacy on mainland Nova Scotia, the Micmac sided with the French, with whom they had been trading for many years. As a countermeasure, the English brought in one hundred Mohawk braves from New York state in 1712.

Farther along Lower Saint George Street is one-time inn and tavern, now the **O'Dell Museum.** The founder of this establishment was once a dispatch rider for a pony express which in 1849 became the Associated Press in New York. Today in this restored inn, you'll find a collection of Victorian costumes, furnishings, and shipbuilding artifacts. Back in the days when the one-time inn catered to cosmopolitan travelers, the best rooms in the house could be had for $1.50 a night. Admission is free. For information call (902) 532–2041. The museum is open daily from June 1 to September 30 from 9:30 A.M. to 5:30 P.M.

A short way farther into town on this same thoroughfare is the **Bailey House,** built in 1780 by an artificer at Fort Anne. It was once the home of wealthy United Empire Loyalists whose social standing was so lofty that they could host a grand ball for the Duke of Kent.

A few blocks farther down the street is the **King's Theatre,** built in 1922. This was the home of Henry Goldsmith, a lawyer and great-grandnephew of playwright Oliver Goldsmith, who wrote *She Stoops to Conquer.* The building is now used as the venue for the Annapolis Royal Arts Festival, held every September, and plays and films are shown here year-round.

Just across the street from the theater is the ❖ **Old Post Office,** the site of which was home to Colonel Samual Vetch, the captor of Port Royal in 1710. Following Confederation, the newly formed government built a chateau-style post office and customs warehouse on the site.

If you happen to be standing at this corner at lunch or dinner time, you may want to break up your tour with a stop at ❖ **Newman's,** also close by. This highly acclaimed gourmet establishment is housed in a pink one-time warehouse on lower St. George Street. Its obscure location belies its renown—it has been written up in many prominent Canadian publications.

The owner/chef, John Gartland, who received his training at the Culinary Institute of America, has worked in France, Germany, and Israel. At Newman's you can get everything from Cajun-style scrumptious blackened fish to lobster, but if you are really feeling adventurous, try a "ragout of black bear with winter vegetables."

Gartland explained that there have been a lot of black bears around these past few years, and some of them have been particularly bothersome. When the Department of Lands and Forests are brought in to put down a bear that is threatening its human neighbors, he buys the bear and uses it for his restaurant. "So it's ecologically responsible," he noted. The surprisingly tender bear meat has the taste of an Oriental or Mongolian dish, since its rather beefy-tasting broth includes Chinese mushrooms.

The restaurant has a lot of artwork on the walls (not for sale) and an eclectic decor. There is a terrace out back where you can dine amid the kitchen's pretty, well-tended herb garden.

Two other houses are worthy of mention: the **Adams-Ritchie House,** dating from 1712; and the **Sinclair Inn,** dating from around 1710 and including elements from three early buildings that served as a hostelry. A silversmith from Quebec, Jean-Baptiste Soulard, kept his shop here.

119

The Adams-Ritchie House, right next to Newman's, used to be the site of government meetings when Annapolis Royal was the provincial capital (before Halifax was founded). One of the Fathers of Confederation, Sir Thomas Ritchie, was born here. The left-hand side of the house is now the home of **Leo's Cafe.** On the right-hand side is an antiques shop with two floors of wonderfully preserved antique porcelain dishware and other fine china. The upper floor also has larger antiques. Downstairs at Leo's Cafe (to the left end of the building), the attraction is a selection of pasta dishes featuring homemade linguini and your choice of sauces in varying degrees of spiciness.

Now that you've been well fed, resume your walk by continuing along the same thoroughfare until you reach ◆ **Fort Anne.** This national historic site represents the fourth and last French fortress built at this site. Only three buildings remain out of sixty that once stood on this spot.

Fort Anne is comprised of pieces of several different forts, dating from different eras and under different countries. From the fort's hilly defenses you will get a nice view of the harbor and a stretch of lowland originally reclaimed by a dike constructed by the Acadians.

The original fort was constructed by the French here in 1643. The powder magazine, which dates from 1708, is the last remnant of the French fortifications. The earthworks, which look like empty moats, have been left in the state in which they were found. They are among the oldest historic features in the entire National Historic Parks System.

If you visit the museum housed in the old field officers' quarters, which the Duke of Kent had constructed in 1797, you can get the whole story of the English-French conflict that raged for many years in this region. One room is dedicated to the story of the Acadian settlers. Other rooms feature collections of old military badges and buttons and lots of antique weaponry.

You will be strolling through Fort Anne's star-shaped fortifications, its beautifully tended lawns and its earthworks dating from 1702. They offer a magnificent view of the basin.

After visiting the fort complex, return to Upper Saint George Street (Lower Saint George Street becomes Upper about halfway through the village) and continue walking past the Military Cemetery and onward past Prince Albert Road until you come to the Annapolis Royal Historic Gardens on your right.

Annapolis Royal has many great things going for it. One of its top attractions has to be without a doubt the ◆ **Annapolis Royal Historic Gardens.** They have been growing in brilliance for twenty-five years now. The ten-acre (4-hectare) gardens are abutted by reclaimed marshland and a wildfowl sanctuary. The gardens contain more than 200 varieties of roses, with a total of 2,000 bushes. Some varieties of these roses were grown by the early Acadian settlers. At their peak, in midsummer, some roses cascade over a huge, rough-hewn log pergola. There is a small replica of an Acadian cottage, complete with a kitchen garden, or potager, containing the ingredients for traditional Acadian soups, or *potage*.

Traditional English gardening is represented in the form of the Governor's Garden, carefully tended in eigthteenth-century style. There is also a Victorian Garden, accented by a 300-year-old elm tree. This is the end point of the Annapolis Royal walking tour's route. Return to your car.

If you cross a small bridge to the village of **Granville Ferry,** you will be entering yet another narrow peninsula similar to Digby Neck, from whence you just came. Pause for a moment after crossing the bridge and look back across the water at Annapolis Royal. On a clear day this has to be one of the prettiest vistas the province has to offer.

Drive southwest on Route 1 for about 6 miles (10 km) and you will come across an old wooden fortress.

This is the ◆ **Habitation** at Port Royal, a re-creation of the oldest European settlement on the continent north of Florida. This was a reconstruction, built in the 1930s, based on the records of the inhabitants of a fur-trading post here that dated back to 1605. Historians have never been able to ascertain the exact site of the original Port Royal, but this is definitely in the ballpark if not right at home base. It was here that the Order of Good Cheer was formed to boost morale during the long winter nights.

Several of the post's inhabitants had literary inclinations, in particular a lawyer named Marc Lescarbot, who wrote copious notes about his year at the site. To amuse the bored pioneers, he created theatrical pieces that were performed for the inhabitants in what he named the Theater of Neptune. This eventually was honored in the selection of a name for Canada's first professional repertory theater, Neptune Theatre, located in Halifax.

**Acadian Cottage at
Annapolis Royal Historic Gardens**

It is because of Lescarbot's notes, and those of Samuel de Champlain and Père Pierre Biard, a Jesuit priest, that historians were able to learn so much about the early days of the Acadians in Nova Scotia. One of the things that strikes the visitor most at this carefully re-created fortress is the size of the beds. The original inhabitants of Port Royal were a stocky lot, with beds that could hardly accommodate Snow White's pals by modern standards. They were also quite elevated and canopied to retain warmth.

The little charcoal-colored rectangular fortress, with its stone-covered central courtyard and rugged furnishings recalling farm settlements from seventeenth-century Normandy, is so startling in its authenticity that it feels like time travel. It is hardly a stretch of the imagination to picture the original traders going about their business in the 1600s. This illusion is helped along by the many costumed interpreters, French-accented Acadians from the local area. Wearing *sabots*—wooden shoes—the interpreters do everything from cutting wood into shingles to maintaining a lookout for enemy attacks. Their clothing is made from hand-woven material carefully sewn in the manner of the original inhabitants.

Be sure to see the fur-trading room, where the wealth of hides and commercial paraphernalia really re-create the feeling of this old fur-trading post.

Leaving Port Royal, backtrack roughly a mile (1.5 km) in the direction of Granville Ferry and then turn left along the Hollow Mountain Road, an unpaved byway that is nevertheless quite passable in dry weather. When you reach the end of this secondary road, you'll be facing the Bay of Fundy. If you turn left again, you will soon be in ◆ **Delap's Cove** (population 65), which has some of the most noteworthy hikes in the province.

It is along this stretch of Fundy coast that the province's unusual prehistoric past is most evident. Basaltic lava flows have hardened into crystals, which have been worn and shaped by the relentless forces of the tide. Anyone who has visited the coast of a volcanic island—for example, the Canary Islands—will instantly recognize the rock formations as the result of hardened lava flows. The only thing that has shaped the lava somewhat differently here is the relentless crashing of the world's highest tides.

Whereas on Digby Neck you will see basalt cliffs leaning precariously like primeval towers of Pisa, here the rocks are sometimes softened into hard, round beach stones or natural basalt pools that fill up at high tide, allowing the brave and hardy to take a chilly dip in the tidal waters.

Delap's Cove is the one-time settlement of freed black slaves from the United States, who lived here on land granted to them by the Crown. Their old farms have now returned to the wilderness, cleft in two by old logging roads.

If you wish to go on a wilderness trek here, plan on at least two hours for the journey. Finding the area's two trails is easy: Simply follow the signs marked DELAP'S COVE WILDERNESS TRAIL. The trails are a little farther up the road than the wharf; if you actually descend to the cove itself, you've gone too far. You can leave your car at the parking lot at the designated trail entrance just before the descent to the cove.

You have a choice between the **Bohaker Trail,** a 2-mile (3.2-km) oval that begins on an escarpment of rocks overlooking the bay; and **Charlie's Trail,** which is a more challenging 2½--mile (3.8-km) loop that starts a mile (1.6 km) or so farther down the rock-strewn logging road. Charlie's Trail requires better hiking boots that offer more stability, since the trail consists of harsh granite terrain. The payoff of taking the easier Bohaker Trail is a 43-foot waterfall at its end point. The Bohaker also allows you the delicate pleasure of salt sea mist mingled with the scent of black spruce.

An alternate walk is simply to follow the coast by walking along the huge basalt boulders that stretch past the government wharf. From here all up along the coast is a daisy chain of fishing wharves and tiny lighthouses that serve the small communities of Delap's Cove, Parker's Cove, Hampton, and Hall's Harbour.

Boats along the coast are tied up flush alongside the wharves at high tide and are left immobilized 20 feet or so below on the sea bottom when the tide goes out. Depending on when the tides are coming in, you may chance upon lobster boats being unloaded. The fishermen will gladly sell you some from right off the boat, if you are interested in boiling your own lobsters, Maritime style.

You can also follow this coast along the unnumbered shore road, turning inland at Hampton or Port Lorne to rejoin Highway 101. Or if you don't want to go that far on an old shore road, you can turn down at Parker's Cove, proceed to the Granville ferry, and cross the small bridge that separates it from Annapolis Royal.

From here you can follow the Evangeline Trail into the Annapolis Valley's rich farmlands, or take a side trip into wilderness at a national park in the center of the province. To do this get onto Route 8 in Annapolis Royal and proceed inland in the direction of ◆ **Kejimkujik National Park.**

If you do opt for the national park, plan to return to the Evangeline Trail, even though it means backtracking. Otherwise you will miss some of the prettiest countryside in this end of the country and some of the finest country inns and restaurants in the area.

Kejimkujik (or Keji, as it is generally called by locals) comprises 147 square miles (381 sq. km) of land, in the center of which is a large lake into which run several rivers. Canoes can be rented by the day or week at the park headquarters in **Maitland Bridge.** Rates for campers are quite reasonable, but spots are in short supply. If you want to explore the park in the daytime but not camp out, consider staying at the **Whitman Inn,** which has been operating nearby for eons. It is a pretty yellow country inn on the right-hand side of the road, just a five-minute drive farther down Route 8 past the park entrance. The Whitman Inn is a restored turn-of-the-century homestead, still with its original furnishings, and boasting a library and parlor with books dating back to the 1800s. For details on this Heritage inn, call 800–690–INNS or (902) 682–2226.

Take note that you have to pick your season well for a visit to Keji. At the tail end of August until the end of the first week in September, it is lovely; but from late spring to early summer, you will be an "all-you-can-eat buffet" on two legs for the ticks and blackflies.

There is a standard campsite at the beginning of the park, in an area called Jeremy's Bay, where people rent sites by the night and prepare for or recover from their forays into the wilderness. For wilderness camping you will be expected to do some planning for your trip when you reserve your canoe, including reserving a designated campsite in the park's interior. Sites are spaced generously apart from one another, allowing for exceptional privacy. Due to the extremely small number of these sites and their enormous popularity, park attendants recommend booking these spots at least sixty days in advance during the summer. In the early fall, my favorite time for Keji, these are far more available, but try to plan ahead anyway.

Be wary of leaving scraps of food lying around or of not carefully disposing of any of the debris of human consumption. The numerous beaver and muskrat that you will see are not the only nonhuman inhabitants of the park. Bears, cougars, and lynxes, not to mention other native Nova Scotian species, also inhabit this park.

Micmac people camped in these lands many centuries before the white man. Petroglyphs that are visible when water washes over them are testimony to their early presence. To see these ancient markings, visitors are advised to check them out with an experienced Micmac guide. Otherwise visitors may inadvertently destroy some of the markings. When I visited, park guides showed me places where people had unknowingly pulled their canoes on shore and scraped and damaged the markings. In other places contemporary visitors carved their names right over petroglyphs, without noticing what they were defacing.

The area where they are found is in a small inlet called Fairy Bay, which is unnamed on the maps displayed at the Information Centre but can be easily picked out by tracing a line from Jakes' Landing, where canoes can be rented, to Merrymakedge, where there are picnic tables. A lookout is indicated midway between these two points, at a spot denoted by the number 12.

This is easily found on the road. A staircase leads to the lookout overlooking Fairy Bay. A trail next to this lookout will lead you to the spot, so getting there is not difficult. Knowing what to look for is another matter; that is where the guides come in.

Historians now know that people lived in Nova Scotia as early as 10,500 years ago, but they have not been able to ascertain whether these early inhabitants were the ancestors of the Micmac who greeted and traded with the white men of the 1600s. The land may have witnessed the visits and passings of many peoples after the Ice Age slowly retreated and the trees and forests returned.

The pictographs that the ancient Micmac left show elements from their nomadic life as hunters and gatherers. Moose are quite clearly depicted, as well as a snakelike creature, possibly Kipika'm, the Horned Serpent Person, a monstrous snake who lives in the Micmac underworld. This character appears in all native legends in Canada, end even in Siberia. Anthropologists theorize that the serpent-creature elements of native oral history go back as far as 11,000 years, back to the original migration from Siberia across the Bering land bridge.

One late summer night after we had canoed far back into Keji, we heard drumming and chanting from far off—some descendants of the original carvers, perhaps?

An apt summary of Keji is that the park itself could easily serve as a destination in itself, for those interested in taking an extended canoe trip into the Nova Scotia of the ancient Micmac.

After Kejimkujik, backtrack to the Evangeline Trail, which you can rejoin at Junction 22, roughly 3 miles (5 km) before you return to Annapolis Royal.

APPLE BLOSSOM COUNTRY

Provincial Highway 101, and its parallel trunk road, Route 1, from Annapolis Royal to Wolfville, run through some of the prettiest countryside you will ever see: rolling hills dotted with apple trees. These days even an occasional vineyard can be seen as grape growing becomes more and more popular.

Sheltered on both its western and eastern sides and lying along the fertile Annapolis River, the Annapolis Valley enjoys a mini-climate all its own. Spring comes earlier here than elsewhere in the province, summers seem warmer and sunnier, and fall holds out the tantalizing possibility of a profusion of gold, red, and fiery orange trees set amid the soft ochre glow of drying grass in the fields, all with warm Indian summer days thrown in. Winter along the coast is often unpredictable, with first a damp cold snowstorm followed by freezing rain and then a thaw. But here in the valley, the effect is often pure Currier and Ives, with snow-topped steeples, gorgeous winter scenery, and cross-country ski trails popping up here and there.

As you wind your way through this beautiful country, be sure to turn off at Exit 16 to visit the ◆ **Oaklawn Farm Zoo.**

"We had no intentions of ever being a zoo," says Gail Rogerson. She and husband Ron, who own and run the Oaklawn Farm Zoo, had always just liked animals. They collected exotic pets on their Aylesford-area farm. For years Gail was a schoolteacher and in 1975, her son's class visited the farm. The visits snowballed, and by the end of the 1970s, dozens of teachers were taking groups of students out to visit the farm.

It reached the point that people would drive up to the farm, insisting that the farm was a public place. Privacy became a thing of the past. "On a nice weekend our drive would be filled with strangers."

Forced to choose between moving away or opening their doors to the public, the Rogersons became the owners of the only zoo east of Montreal that features exotic animals like lemurs, Japanese macaques, a gibbon (which you can hear from a long way off), camels, and a yak. You could spend hours watching the monkeys fooling around. Kids like the llamas. Several lions live here in spacious quarters, and many of the animals range freely in large, open fields.

The zoo has a canteen where you can take a break from the hot midday sun, coin-operated vending machines where you can obtain snacks for feeding sheep and other small animals, and a gift shop in the two-story, log-cabin reception building that features wild-animal sweatshirts and local crafts.

Be sure to check out the reception building's animal-head carvings on its second floor. Ten of the carvings are on the rounded ends of the joists. A cougar comes out of the end of two wall logs, while an owl stands out in bas relief. Every carving represents an animal at the zoo, including resident and pet Badness the Pug.

The carvings are so subtly crafted that they trick the eye such that you have to look for them. Make a point of looking closely at the log ends and you will see a gibbon, an alligator, a llama, and a host of other critters. The carvings are the work of artist John Murray, who used a Haida Indian knife, traditionally used to make totem poles. Along with other artful pieces, the building has an-almost-life-size papier-mâché zebra crafted by another local artist.

The Rogersons remind visitors that the principal concern of the farm is not to exhibit the animals but to provide a home for them where they can be at ease and breed. The zoo breeds registered dogs as well as exotic animals for sale to other zoos. Many of these animals are endangered in the wild, so their only hope of survival is through zoos and wildlife refuges. Oaklawn Farm is open from April to November, with May and June weekdays the favorite times for school visits. Admission is $3.50 for adults; seniors and students, $2.50; and age twelve and under pay $2.00. For information call (902) 847–9790.

If you decide to pick a few mussels and drift along the shore for a bit, take a side road out of Aylesford back toward the Bay of Fundy shore. Head toward **Morden** or Victoria Harbour on the secondary road out of Aylesford. Along the shore, in Morden, you will come to a stone cross, a monument erected to honor the Acadians who once hid out here during the winter of 1755, away from the British who were busily expelling their compatriots. Their food consisted of meat and mussels provided by their Micmac allies. In 1790 their descendants erected a church and plastered its walls with powdered mussel shells.

All along this road between the valley and the Fundy coast you have been zigzagging the North Mountain range. This was formed 200 million years ago at a time when the supercontinent began splitting into smaller continents. At that time rifts opened up between the sandy plain around the Cobequid Hills of Truro, and basaltic lava was spewed out from the Earth's belly, spilling out into the area. As it cooled, the North Mountain ridge was formed from the fractures and tilting, along with the rock formations of Digby Neck. The most spectacular result to come from this era of upheaval, apart from the Bay of Fundy itself, is the headland that overlooks the Minas Channel. It is known as ✤ **Cape Split.** This is the legendary home of the great Micmac god, Glooscap.

To get into the rugged-nature spirit of things, the vigorous among you may want to make the trek to the end of Cape Split. This is the must-do trek for Nova Scotia's committed hikers, since the spectacular panorama offered by the end point of this excursion is unmatched anywhere else in the province. Count on needing a day's recovery from this trek, so plan to stay either at Blomidon Park, where you can camp, or at a nearby bed-and-breakfast establishment. To get to Cape Split, stay on Highway 101 until you reach Exit 11 just outside Wolfville. Turn onto Route 358 and drive north in the direction of Scots Bay and Cape Blomidon.

If you are planning on finding overnight accommodations close to Cape Split, the closest place is the ✤ **Planter's Barracks Country Inn,** on the Starr's Point Road (also known as Route 358) in **Port Williams** as you head to the cape. It's a historic inn in every sense of the word. It dates back to 1778, when it was part of Fort Hughes.

To get to Planter's Barracks, turn off Highway 101 at Exit 11 onto Route 358. From there continue to Port Williams and turn right at the set of flashing lights. You can't miss the inn. The building has the look of an old English country manor house.

Inside are Nova Scotia antiques. There are nine guest rooms with full bath and shower; one room has a fireplace. English-style afternoon tea is served, and there is plenty of room here on the terrace and in the gardens to recover from Cape Split excursions. For reservations call (902) 542-7879.

Just past Port Williams on Route 358, you'll come to Starr's Point and the historic ✤ **Prescott House,** which was built in 1814–16 by Charles Prescott. He was a successful merchant who served as a member of the legislature for Cornwallis Township in the early 1800s. His true claim to fame, however, is apples.

Prescott was the man who introduced the Gravenstein apple and other superior apple varieties to Nova Scotia, forever changing the landscape of the Annapolis Valley. In his day all ornamentals, fruits, and vegetable and fodder crops came from European stock or were adapted to the eastern United States. Because of the harsh winters and proximity to the ocean, some did not succeed here until Prescott established strains that thrived in the Nova Scotian climate.

The honorary member of the horticultural societies of New York, Boston, and London offered grafting stock, in the way of ". . . scions and buds of any kind to every person who may apply in the proper season . . . ," according to a notice posted by Prescott himself.

The impressive Georgian architecture of Prescott House is complemented by the period furnishings that Prescott's great-granddaughter collected when she restored the house in the 1930s. Surrounding the house are beautiful trees, gardens, and lawns. The vista includes the diked lands of the Cornwallis River. For more information call (902) 542–3984.

Prescott House is open from the beginning of June to mid-October. Hours are Monday to Saturday from 9:30 A.M. to 5:30 P.M. and Sunday from 1:00 to 5:30 P.M. Admission is free.

Pause at a point on Route 358 called **The Lookoff,** high on North Mountain, for a spectacular view of Minas Basin, site of the highest of the Bay of Fundy's record-breaking tides. There is adequate space here for parking, as well as washrooms and picnic tables, so you can take in the scenery while you munch. Sprawling below like a scattered bouquet you can see apple orchards, woodlots, lazy cows drifting through fields of clover, old farmhouses, and, farther back, spread out like a brown carpet, the muddy waters of the basin.

From this point continue a little past **Scots Bay,** where a walk of slightly more than 5 miles (8 km) begins. In June the red trillium blooms along this path. Far below you can watch eagles and hawks soaring above the sea.

There is another hike in this area, slightly more than 10 miles (17 km) long. This hike starts at the campground at **Cape Blomidon,** atop the eroding sandstone cliffs, and then backtracks in a loop through woodlands.

Like the Cape Split hike, this trail demands extreme caution, as erosion is slowly claiming the cliffs. The edge of the headland is dangerous; no barriers are there to protect people from falling to the beach 330 feet (100 m) or so below the footpath. Several times along this path, the trail diverges to the edge, over which the incautious could plunge to their doom.

Whatever you do, don't whiz past this area quickly after your Cape Split excursion or a visit to Blomidon. Since it is set deep in the heart of a rich agricultural area, with trendy flavorings from the local university, the stretch of road from Kentville to Wolfville has much to offer the gourmet.

If you are there at the right time of year—that is, the third weekend in May—you must take in the Annapolis Valley's ◆ **Apple Blossom Festival.** Even if you hardly take in any of the festival events, the scenery here at the end of May is breathtaking. There will be mile after mile of orchards in full bloom and beautiful spring weather. You can also enjoy an assortment of stately old homes for bed-and-breakfasting as well as gourmet restaurants in the college town of Wolfville. **Chez La Vigne** and **Tattingstone** are particularly noteworthy eateries.

THE GLOOSCAP TRAIL

From this point in the valley, you can easily drive back to Halifax, via Windsor. But if you have already visited Halifax and are heading out of the province, you may want to try following a route referred to as the **Glooscap Trail.** This nears the shores of Minas Basin, the inner arm of the Bay of Fundy. It is a pretty, unspoiled area, accessed by leaving Provincial Highway 101 at Exit 5 in Windsor and driving along Trunk Highway 215.

It is with this routing that I will take you out of the province. (If you do drive back to Halifax, you can always rejoin the Glooscap Trail in Truro 60 miles (100 km), past Halifax toward New Brunswick). To do this take Exit 14A or 15 off Provincial Highway 102 outside Truro to Route 2.

If you travel the considerably less-traveled Route 215, you will be edging the area of the world's highest tides, which reach their peak of 53 feet (16 m) at Burnt Coat Head near Noel. Just a few minutes' drive farther down the road and you will reach **Maitland,** which is the entry spot for ◆ **rafting on the**

131

tidal wave, otherwise known as a bore, for 18 miles (29 km) up the Shubenacadie River aboard Zodiacs, big, inflated dingy-type boats. The entire trip takes half a day, during which time you are pushed upriver by "roller-coaster" rapids of 3 to 10 feet (1 to 3 m). Lunch is included.

Two outfits take rafters on this trip. One, called **Tidal Bore Rafting,** is run by Bill MacKay, who you can contact at (902) 755–0899. The other is simply called **Rafting** and is operated by Hilbert and Eppie Knol. Their toll-free number is (800) 565–RAFT; local numbers are (902) 758–4032, (902) 758–4066, and (902) 758–2177. Rates for both outfits, per trip, are $45 per adult. Children under twelve go for $35.

The first highlight of the road after Truro is in **Portaupique,** where you can pay a visit to the studio and gallery of a noted artist named Joy Laking. You may have seen some of her prints in other areas of the province, particularly in shops that specialize in Bass River chairs. This is, no doubt, because **Bass River** is just 3 miles (5 km) down the road from the ✪ **Joy Laking Gallery.** Laking's work is comprised of watercolors and serigraphs of a decidedly nostalgic nature—sunny front porches on hazy summer afternoons, lady's slippers and trilliums, and kitchen curtains blowing softly in a summer breeze, all painted with delicacy and liveliness. In Portaupique you will also find the remains of an Acadian dike, along the saltmarsh that edges the shore.

Apart from its obvious appeal to beachcombers, the rugged Fundy shore of Nova Scotia has much to offer would-be geologists and other rockhounds. The areas of coastline that front on the Bay of Fundy have a wealth of prehistoric fossils just waiting to be gathered like so many wild berries.

If you take a close look at your official "Scenic Travelways" map (available at any tourism information booth), you will note the fossil icons that dot the shores of the Bay of Fundy. They indicate the richest areas for fossil exploration.

Roughly 350 million years ago, long before dinosaurs began decorating kids' pajamas, this area was teeming with life. Lying near the equator, it was wedged between North America and Africa, in the middle of the supercontinent called Pangaea. As the continents started drifting apart, huge rift valleys formed, of which the Bay of Fundy is one. As the tides coursed through this cleft in the continents, water eroded a huge cross-section, revealing a window into the world of 200 million years ago and beyond.

The area of the Bay of Fundy is noted as the world's best site of continuously exposed Late Carboniferous Age rocks. Along these same shores are exposed sea cliffs that reveal ancient treasures from the Triassic and Jurassic geological periods. And you would never think of Nova Scotia as a place full of volcanoes, but along these shores you will quite unexpectedly come across rock formations created by ancient lava flows.

The fossilized legacy of some of the world's oldest terrestrial reptiles and the oldest land-dwelling snails have been found along here. Two hundred million years ago, some of the planet's first dinosaurs roamed the desert that was Nova Scotia. And 70,000 years ago mastodons were here. Bones of two mastodons, including a baby, were recently found in a gypsum pit near Halifax.

Apart from rugged basalt cliffs and fossils, the area has other geological delights, noted and treasured for centuries by the native peoples. Micmac Indian legend has it that the mighty Glooscap lived across the narrow neck of the **Minas Basin,** in the area of Blomidon and Cape Split, the breathtaking promontory that overlooks the spot where tides reach 50 feet (16 m) and more. From there the great god of the Micmac looked over his children.

Once he was mocked by an animal spirit named Beaver, and his anger caused him to scoop up land from the gorges and fling the clods of earth at the mocking spirit, creating islands that now comprise ◆ **Five Islands Provincial Park,** near Economy, and scattering the jewels, known today as jasper, agate, onyx, and amethyst. To this day the legendary gifts of Glooscap draw rockhounds from around the world to the shores of the Bay of Fundy.

At Five Islands Provincial Park, on Route 2, you will find camping, a beach, and, of course, five islands: **Moose, Diamond, Long, Egg,** and **Pinnacle.**

The picnic areas and the **Estuary Nature Trail** in this park are marked with interpretive displays explaining the geology of the site.

In the **Parrsboro** area you'll meet a lot of geology buffs and rockhounds. The pleasant little town of some 1,600 people is

133

actually the biggest community along this route, so this is the place to stock up on film or food before exploring the area's coastline. The rockhounds you will meet will be looking for zeolites—semiprecious stones like amethyst and agate.

At the ✦ **Fundy Geological Museum,** on Two Island Road in Parrsboro, you can take a guided tour that covers the fossil and mineral wealth of the area. Operated by the local geological society, the tours cost $5.00 per person or $15.00 for families. They are usually held on Saturday, during which time people visit either mineral sites or fossil sites on a guided collecting tour. This museum also holds lapidary workshops where you can learn about the geological formations.

The fossil deposits are from two different eras, and the basalt areas feature the various minerals. The Saturday guided tours take visitors to only one of the sites per tour, so if your interests are quite specific, it's best to call ahead to determine which area is slated for a visit.

Wear sturdy hiking boots with good ankle support. Collectors are permitted to take just those fossils or zeolites that they find on the beach, not rocks extracted from the cliffs, where only geologists and palaeontologists are permitted to work.

People touring the beach areas should pack a sweater, because when the fog rolls in, the temperature can drop quite suddenly. The beaches can also subject you to a considerable amount of solar radiation as the light reflects off the basalt cliffs, so good sun protection and a hat are advised. For information call (902) 254–3814.

The other highlight along this coast is **Joggins,** which can be reached via two routes after Parrsboro. Route 2 turns inland, leaving you with the choice of a small highway (number 209), which skirts the remainder of Fundy coast, or traveling inland along Route 2 and either skipping Joggins altogether or backtracking to Joggins via Exit 4, some 13 miles (20 km) from Amherst, and then driving to Joggins on Highway 242.

Joggins is a must if you want to get to the bottom of fossils' mysterious appeal. When you reach the village, turn onto Main Street in beautiful downtown Joggins (population 491), where you will find the ✦ **Joggins Fossil Centre.** Guides here will take the time to explain the origins of the area's many 350-million-year-old fossilized trees, ferns, insects, amphibians, and animal tracks. The center is open from June 1 to the end of September and has an extensive collection of fossils on site. For more information write to the Joggins Fossil Centre, Main Street, Joggins, N.S. B0L 1A0; or phone (902) 251–2727 in season, or off-season (902) 251–2618.

After Joggins you have merely a 12-mile (20-km) drive to the border, where your travels through Nova Scotia will be complete.

CAPE BRETON

1. *An Drochaid*
2. The Mull
3. Inverness Miners' Museum
4. Margaree River/Margaree Salmon Museum
5. Scarecrow Theatre
6. Le Motif
7. Sunset Art Gallery
8. Chéticamp Island
9. Cape Breton Highlands National Park
10. Lone Shieling
11. Keltic Lodge
12. Lynn Gorey's Craft Shop and Art Gallery
13. Giant MacAskill Museum
14. Lobster Galley at Harbour House
15. Gaelic College of Celtic Arts and Crafts
16. Alexander Graham Bell Museum
17. Bald eagles/Amoeba's Sailing Tours
18. Gisele's Country Inn
19. Telegraph House
20. Uisage Bann Falls
21. Highland Village
22. Cossit House/Jost House
23. Old Mira Trading Post
24. Sydney and Louisbourg Railway Station Museum
25. Fortress Louisbourg
26. The Big Pond Festival
27. Wallace MacAskill Museum
28. LeNoir Forge Museum

CAPE BRETON

While the residents of Prince Edward Island are still undecided about the possible disruption caused by a "fixed link" with the rest of the world, Cape Bretoners have no such worries. Linked to the mainland of Nova Scotia by the world's deepest causeway since 1955, it remains very much an island, in every sense of the word.

Here "bilingual" could just as easily mean Gaelic and English as French and English, although all these cultures plus Micmac are strongly evident on Cape Breton Island. The Micmac, of course, have been here for more than ten thousand years. Today, visitors will spot posters proclaiming "The Champion Returns", meaning fiddle champion Lee Creemo, a Micmac from the shores of the Bras d'Or Lake.

Scots came in two basic waves of immigration. After the failed rebellion of 1745, many Highlanders chose Cape Breton as their exile and refuge. Then, in the 1820s, many landlords drove the Scottish tenants off their land and took it over as sheep pasture. The landless Scots left for Cape Breton and points beyond, in search of a place where they could continue to live as their ancestors had.

The French actually settled Cape Breton before the Scots, but were then exiled after the fall of Louisbourg, their stronghold. After this many of them returned to France. A few years later they returned to Cape Breton and settled in communities only a few miles from the Scots.

At every gas station and rest stop on Cape Breton you will see locally produced books, stories of the first Scottish settlers or the French, and in among the stack of videotapes, heavily in demand by visitors awed by the island's spectacular scenery, you will find cassette tapes of Cape Breton's native sons and daughters who have managed to carve out their own niche in the music industry with a blend of Celtic traditional and modern rock ballads.

HOME OF THE CEILIDH

You will be short-changing yourself if you do not take the time to enjoy firsthand the music and arts that have kept a love of Cape Breton culture foremost even in the hearts of the island's economic exiles who have drifted off to central Canada in search of opportunity.

Eleanor Mullendor, Mabou innkeeper, as well as the neighbor and sometime spokesperson of the musical Rankin family, points out that there is a local festival somewhere on the island at least once a week all summer long. Along the boardwalk that skirts the waterfront of Chéticamp, near the start of the Cabot Trail, one has a chance of catching live performances three times a week. If you happen to spend any length of time in one place you may also be lucky enough to get invited to a traditional Gaelic party, or *ceilidh,* at someone's home. If that happens, you're in for a special treat, a holdover from the descendants of the hardy group of pioneers who left the hard times and persecution of Scotland to establish a New Scotland for themselves on Cape Breton Island.

With that in mind, the very first thing to do once you cross the Causeway is to buy a copy of the local paper, *The Cape Breton Post,* turn to the entertainment section, and scan the listings, planning your itinerary accordingly. Then fill up your tank before leaving **Port Hastings** and turn left onto Route 19, to head north along the scenic western coast.

In short order you will come to **Judique** (the Judiques, to be exact, since there are supposedly ten of them, including North Judique, South Judique, Big Judique, Little Judique, not to mention the Centre, Banks, Chapel, Ponds, and Rear and Intervale Judiques). Along the shore road in this area you will find a number of wharves where you can purchase lobsters straight from the boats.

A short drive farther up Route 19 will bring you to a sign indicating a left turn to get to Port Hood, where a public wharf serves more lobster fishermen. If you continue on Route 19 from this junction, you will soon come to **Mabou,** its most recent claim to fame proudly proclaimed by a small, tastefully painted billboard along the side of the road: a portrait of fresh-faced native sons and daughters, now become international recording stars. "Welcome to Mabou, home of the Rankins," it proclaims.

The pride that Mabou's inhabitants feel in the young singers' success is at least partially due to their skill in taking Gaelic singing to the masses, once again putting the spotlight on Mabou as a center of Gaelic language and traditional culture.

In a small, part-time museum called **The Bridge,** or, in Gaelic, **⬦ An Drochaid,** eager youngsters line up for fiddle lessons. Located near the bridge on the only piece of highway in the village, the museum also offers day-camp courses in Gaelic, with children from far afield taking the opportunity to learn the ancient language, which reportedly is spoken by more people here than in Scotland. Mabou is a small place, with a population just over 300, and so serene that it seems quite likely that very little has changed here in the last several decades. It is peaceful, restful, serene, and unhurried.

Take a look at Mabou from the front deck of the **Duncreigan Inn** (located just south of the village proper and across the bridge from the community). One has a perfect view of the tiny village church, reflected perfectly in the still water. It is easy to imagine a life here where time stands still, even though the village has international recording stars living cheek-by-jowl with the bald eagles and the moose. Eleanor Mullendor sometimes organizes a *ceilidh* for her guests at the inn, inviting local performers and Gaelic-speaking seniors for a "milling frolic," so it's worth asking if one of these events is being planned.

Mabou pioneers were determined not to yield to persecution in their homelands. The Scottish settlers who came to this end of Cape Breton and succeeded in making a life of it were of the most hardy stock. Think of it as Pioneers' Darwinism. Those who did not succeed moved on. At one point 800 of the Scottish pioneers left Cape Breton en masse for New Zealand, for example. Those who remained and thrived were the toughest of the lot.

Their memory is preserved in the **Our Lady of Seven Sorrows Pioneers Shrine,** which looks for all the world like a simple country church from the patio of the Duncreigan Inn, across the little bridge of the village. It's a surprising optical trick. From the outside, it seems almost too small to accommodate the congregation. But inside, the Douglas fir timbers used to make columns and the skillfully constructed archways make it look like a tiny cathedral.

You can trace the roots of this region's Scottish settlers at the same An Drochaid where fiddle lessons are held. It houses the **Mabou Gaelic and Historical Society Museum.** Admission is free. Information about hours can be had by calling (902) 945–2311.

For a village this size, one can find a remarkable chowder, along with other typical Maritime delicacies, at ◆ **The Mull,** situated on the main road. The settlers of this area came from the Isle of Mull in Scotland. Near here you will find the Mull

140

River. A random sampling of chowders from throughout the island came up with the Mull's chowder as the top choice. The restaurant also sells big rings of Mabou cheese and other local products. (For more on that, the adventurous should read on.)

The Mull was started by innkeepers Eleanor and Charles Mullendor several years before their inn, the Duncreigan, got off the ground. The Mullendors hail originally from Connecticut. They discovered the spot when they came north for a holiday. Before long they bought a 120-acre farm nearby, settled there, and became citizens. They bring their love affair with their chosen homeland into their work, filling the inn with local handicrafts, along with paintings by the province's artists, some of which are for sale.

The inn itself is a modern building, with all the newest comforts, although it was designed to incorporate features of the older farmhouse that the Mullendors originally bought along with their land. At one time it was a charming old home, says the innkeeper, but it had reached the point where as the locals put it, the building was "after falling down."

At one point the Mullendors headed the local arts council for the Inverness area. They have developed considerable contacts with area artists. In every room in the inn, you will find old-time Chéticamp hooked rugs, colored with organic dyes in the traditional manner. They also prepare special meals for their guests, including local Mabou cheeses and *maraq*, also known as "poor man's haggis," a combination of suet, onions, and oatmeal done up like sausage meat in a cow's intestine. Reportedly, it's not a process for the unambitious cooks among us. Rooms can be reserved by calling (800) 840–2207, or by writing Box 59, Mabou, N.S. B0E 2T0. Rates are moderate.

There are several interesting walks in the area. If you turn toward the sea just before crossing the bridge to exit the village, you can follow the Harbour Road to **Mabou Harbour Mouth.** At the tip of land you will find the Mabou Mines lighthouse. From here, provided it hasn't been too rainy, you can walk along the shore for a good distance north, in the direction of Sight Point. Once thriving, Mabou's mines eventually had to be abandoned when the ore that could be reached safely became depleted and digging under the water became impossible.

There is a tiny, pretty lighthouse at **Mabou Mines.** For the vigorous among you, the walk is about 7 or 8 miles (11–13 km) in length, and will take you to Sight Point, where you can rejoin a road that leads north to Inverness.

Another good hike, this time inland, is in a protected stand of forest wilderness, owned by a local historian. The **MacFarlane Woods Nature Reserve** was settled by the MacFarlanes in the 1820s, but they never cut the trees of the hilltop. There you will find a mature maple, beech, and yellow birch forest of a type that covered much of this area before the arrival of the white man.

To get to the woods, cross the village's bridge in the direction of Port Hood, and take the first left along the Mabou Ridge Road. A sign will direct you to **Glencoe Mills Hall.** The woods are marked. An access trail leads up to the top of the hill, where you will see trees, some of which are as big as 3 feet (1 m) in diameter and 100 feet (30 m) high. In early summer you will find rare wild orchids, along with wood sorrel, starflower, and bunchberry. Later in the season the ground will be dotted with wild mushrooms.

When you return to Mabou, you can detour to the **Mabou Pioneers Cemetery** by turning left instead of right at the intersection of Route 19 and the Mabou Ridge Road, and then turning right at the West Mabou Road. Just after the West Mabou Sports Club and Hall, turn right toward **Indian Point,** which overlooks the harbor. Here you will find the old graveyard of the village's pioneers, punctuated by a cairn, a traditional stone marker, and neat rows of headstones of the area's founders, who came here in the early 1800s. The church in the village originally stood here; it was moved to its current location in 1967.

When it's time to leave Mabou, return to Route 19 headed north and follow the signs for **Inverness.** Just outside of town you will see a sign indicating a provincial picnic park. Just after this the road passes over two rivers. The second of these is fed by the **Glenora Falls,** a walk of 0.2 mile (.4 km) in from the road.

After a brief drive you will come to Inverness. You will notice that after several miles of driving in the interior, you are now along the coast again, and even though you have stayed on the same stretch of highway, you will have made a right turn just as you entered the village.

To your left is a pristine but exposed beach, overlooking the Gulf of St. Lawrence, reached by a small boardwalk. On the other side of the street is a number of craft shops, featuring items from as far afield as Chéticamp and Judique; they range from tartans to hooked rugs.

To stock up on film or medical needs before your next scenic excursion, you will find a pharmacy on your right almost as soon as you enter "town" which basically consists of a small stretch of Route 19 that runs along the coast. People in town will direct you to **Freeman's Pharmacy,** but if you look for the sign, you will never find it, as most of the letters are missing. The pharmacy is quite fascinating. There is a large stock of books on local Gaelic culture and history as well as scenic photography volumes and cassettes of all the fiddling greats on the counter next to the cash register.

Backtrack about a block from the intersection that brought you into town and then drive down toward the government wharf. You will notice a small, old-style railway station that has been converted into the ❖**Inverness Miners' Museum.** Outside you will see a cairn, upon which are noted the names of men who died in various mine disasters in the local area before mining was completely abandoned in the 1940s. The museum is open from May to mid-October. Admission is free. (Inquire locally about the hours of operation.)

The railway station itself was built in 1901, during Inverness's salad days, when mining was the town's economic mainstay. About twenty years ago the village's historical society turned it into a museum. It also contains a small archive and displays artwork and photography on a rotating basis.

If you happen to be in Inverness on a Thursday in July or August, take a room in any of the establishments that line the road on the beach side of town and attend the *ceilidh* at the Fire Hall, which starts at 8:00 P.M. The last week in July, there is always the Inverness Gathering, where the *ceilidh* spirit will prevail.

Leaving Inverness, continue for a short way along the coast on Route 19. You'll come to a fork in the road at Dunveigan. From here you have the option of continuing along the scenic coastline on a secondary highway, Route 219, or traveling the more modern stretch of highway that leads to **Southwest Margaree.** There are a number of Margarees in this area of beautiful rolling hills and meadows, and the scenery is just as lovely as it is along the coastline.

143

Of note is the ✦**Margaree River,** which in 1991 was designated as a Canadian Heritage River. It is excellent for salmon fishing. You'll see many anglers as you drift along its banks, should you decide to hike in this area. If you want to make an entire vacation of fishing, the Margaree would fit the bill very well.

Continue inland from Margaree Forks into Northeast Margaree. There you can explore the collection of angling and salmon paraphernalia at the ✦**Margaree Salmon Museum,** to find out just how special the river is for fishing. Their phone number is (902) 248–2848. They are just .2 mile (.3 km) off the Cabot Trail.

A strange thing happens on this stretch of highway. Within a few miles the family names change from MacDonald and Mac-Master to Doucet and LeBlanc. Gaelic heritage starts to give way to French Acadian and, just at the Margarees, the transition seems to be at its high point.

It's surprising when you think of it: Two generations ago, just south of Margaree, people lived and worked in Gaelic. To this day their children learn the traditional songs and attend Gaelic classes. And then, just a short stretch of road away, the language changes to French. How can it have happened that these two cultures managed to survive in a largely English-speaking province?

One gentleman I met provided a few clues. Back in the days of one-room schoolhouses, before buses brought children to their classes, a young pupil's study was at the mercy of the elements. As soon as the bad weather commenced, many children couldn't manage the walk of several miles that going to school meant. So they kept up speaking only the language of their forefathers, being educated largely at home during the long winter months. So in the space of a few miles one would find areas so heavily populated by transplanted highland Scots that you would swear you were in Scotland, and then, isolated by rough roads and bad weather, another whole community of people who continued to speak the French of their ancestors.

Any way you look at it, the impact is a rich cultural stew.

THE CABOT TRAIL

Continue along Route 19 north after Margaree Forks until you rejoin the **Cabot Trail** at **Margaree Harbour.** (If you took the coastal route, you're already there.) On both sides of this harbor are pleasant, uncrowded beaches. Beyond the harbor is a small bridge that promptly brings you to **Belle Cote.** From here on you will encounter a string of thriving Acadian communities.

Just after the road passes a piece of coast that appears to jut out into the gulf, look to your right. A weathered "old barn," which appears to be propped up on one side by poles, has an unusual group of individuals standing around not doing anything in particular. These are the scarecrows of **Cap LeMoine** (on some maps this appears as its English translation: Monk's Hat).

There are more than one hundred scarecrows in all, including a golfer scarecrow. The proprietor of this ◆ **Scarecrow Theatre** has capitalized on these cool lawn ornaments to draw business for a take-out and gift shop that he runs on the same site. It's worth stretching your legs to take a look around, but if you're busy looking at the coast, you could easily miss it.

Continue up the road for a few minutes and you will come to **St. Joseph du Moine.** In this little village you will notice a small art gallery named, imaginatively, **La Bella Mona Lisa.** You can't miss it: The facade is decorated with a massive folk-art painting of a cow in red sneakers. Inside, there are all manner of tongue-in-cheek objets d'art, a lot of them involving cows. There are also gift items like wind chimes, and locally made duck decoys that are too pretty to use.

A short drive from here is **Chéticamp,** population 979. It is the largest Acadian community in the area and the location of the hospital and other essential services such as a pharmacy. Because of this, it seems much more of a town than a village. During the summer months large numbers of French-speaking visitors come here from the rest of the Maritimes. Also roughly 20 percent of its total visitors come from Quebec. In summer, this influx of French-speaking visitors gives it the atmosphere of a surprisingly cosmopolitan village.

The origins of Chéticamp are not entirely straightforward. Although unmistakably French in character, the village's earliest settlers were actually from the French-speaking Channel Islands, under the British Crown. Following the Treaty of Paris in 1763, the French were forced to abandon the fishery in the Gulf of St. Lawrence.

Quickly filling the vacuum was Charles Robin, a French Huguenot from the Isle of Jersey. And at about that time, exiled

Acadians were starting to come back to these shores. The exiles from here had been packed off to St. Malo in France, a port just south of Jersey. Robin offered them work, and soon a thriving community of returned Acadians sprang up. For many years afterward the people of Chéticamp were tied to the fortunes of the Robin family. (They weren't the only Acadians to have dealings with the Jersey "French": On the southeastern coast of Cape Breton, you will find other relics of the Jersey connection, in St. Peters and Arichat.)

Just before reaching Chéticamp proper, you'll see a sign indicating **L'Auberge Doucet,** or Doucet Inn, which is set far back off the road at the end of a massive sloping lawn that would make a good bunny slope at a ski school. Just behind the inn is an unspoiled view of the Cape Breton Highlands. This is your best bet for a quiet place to stay in Chéticamp, which is less than a mile (1 km) farther down the road. Rates are standard. From the patio that separates the two parts of the inn, you can see a small inlet and then, off in the distance, Chéticamp Island. Phone them at (902) 224–3438.

The **Coopérative Artisanale de Chéticamp Ltée** is the first eating establishment that you will encounter as you enter Chéticamp. It is marked by three flags outside: the Canadian maple leaf, the Nova Scotian St. Andrew's cross, and the Acadian tricolor with a star, which you have no doubt seen all over New Brunswick.

Here you can eat a traditional Acadian meal (such as a meat pie) and then check out the craft co-op on the other wing of the same building. On display are excellent examples of Chéticamp hooked rugs. These are so intricately executed that they look more like needlepoint than the usual hooked rug one finds in hobby shops.

The morning that I visited, a lady named Claudette Leblanc demonstrated the rug-hooking technique that developed in Chéticamp as a way of covering the cold wooden floors of the simple Acadian homesteads. As sometimes happens when necessity and isolation conspire, an original art form developed from the use of objects at hand. At first women used burlap potato sacks, stretched out on a frame and pulled tight. Starting with rags and then moving on to wool yarn, the women drew the fabric through the holes in the burlap, forming a loop. They followed a pattern that had been drawn or stamped on the bags. When all of the intricate pattern had been filled in, the stretcher was loosened and the burlap relaxed. This caused the wool loops to be tightly enclosed by the burlap, and a beautifully patterned rug would result.

Several decades ago some women from New York discovered the Chéticamp rugs and started buying them for resale in the United States. There they gained considerable popularity.

There is an amusing story about the start of the hooked-rug cottage industry. One of the early developers of the technique was a woman who was quite noted for the designs she stamped on the burlap backing. As a young girl she had made her materials from rags that she had cut from family clothing. Eventually, the industry became lucrative and her entire family became involved in it, sons as well as daughters. But as the matriarch who started them off aged, she became more and more determined to produce the rag carpets, so much so that the family had to hide all scissors and fabric from her. She passed away at age eighty-nine, still eager to cut rags at every opportunity.

The home she spent her life in is a Heritage Property, out of which a craft shop called ✦ **Le Motif** operates. It is painted a deep blue and is located at the northern end of town. The specialty here, not surprisingly, is rag rugs.

Several restaurants operate down along the boardwalk that follows the waterfront from the government wharf to the end of the village's main drag. You can sit in the **Harbour Restaurant** and watch the lobster boats drift off to cast their traps.

Just past Le Motif you will notice that the village is thinning out as you head north. At this point, on your left, you will see a large, brightly painted sign for the ✦ **Sunset Art Gallery** and an arrow indicating a small wooden building across the street. This is the studio of Bill Roach, one of the province's most noted folk artists. You can't miss his calling: He has a fence made out of people who resemble giant clothes pegs. In the back of the studio, it looks like someone is splitting wood for the fire. A stout woman, carved from a substantial tree trunk, seems ready to shake your hand. Inside, the brightly colored ornaments most frequently are animal friends.

Roach's works are displayed at the Nova Scotia Art Gallery. One was sent to the Canadian Embassy in Washington. D.C., for a six-month period. His wife, Linda, runs the gallery, and she proudly

Folk Art at Sunset Art Gallery

displays photographs of his many commissions, some of which have been sent as far away as Australia.

One woman had the master craftsman produce likenesses of all four of her dogs, from detailed photographs that she had sent him of their front, side, and back views. Then she decided to have her husband done, but all she provided of her spouse for Roach to produce this work of art was a single wallet-size snapshot. But judging by the photo of the final product, it was enough for a lively depiction of the fellow.

You might also want to visit ✦ **Chéticamp Island.** For many years this island was in the hands of the Robin family (known locally as "the Jerseys"), until in 1893 a priest and activist Father Pierre Fiset, arranged the purchase of the island. This was one of many actions undertaken by Fiset in his struggle to lessen the hold of the Robin merchant family on the village.

From the road that runs along the harbor side of Chéticamp Island, you can get a charming view of the village, punctuated by the large church of St.-Pierre, all set against the backdrop of the highlands. The view of the village and the church (built under the direction of Père Fiset) is well worth the trip to the island.

There are only a few houses and cottages on Chéticamp Island, but some of them have an unusual history, recounted to me by Wilbert Aucoin, the owner of one of them. Aucoin is a friendly gentleman who, after retiring from the Royal Canadian Mounted Police, returned to his native Chéticamp, where he now rents out Icelandic horses during the summer months. The house he bought after his retirement had at one time been located in the area designated in the 1930s to become the Highlands National Park. At that time, it was decided that all the houses in the area had to be moved, by barge, up the Chéticamp River and into Chéticamp village. Just as they were pulling one house into the harbor, a big gust of wind blew up, followed by a large wave. The house, which may not have been very securely tied, went under the water. Aucoin remembers watching, along with most of the village, as the house was hoisted out of the water and deposited on the island. Many years later he bought the very same house that had sunk during moving.

Icelandic horses are growing in popularity because of their four-beat gait, which offers a stable, relaxing ride. On this island the people who rent Aucoin's horses have in addition to the nice ride a chance to view eagles, cormorants, cliffs, moorlands, a lighthouse, and beaches. Riders are accompanied by an experienced guide, who can also give some instruction. To reserve call (902) 224–3232. Wilbert's wife, Ruth, manages the reservations.

Apart from checking out the village's thriving crafts and arts community, a warm summer day in Chéticamp is best spent strolling along the boardwalk, where there are free concerts three times a week in summer. Once you've fulfilled your need for human company, follow the road leading out of the village at its northern end, towards the ◆ **Cape Breton Highlands National Park.** Be sure to bring something along to munch, because eating establishments are few and far between along the route you will follow, and you may find yourself getting hungry several hours before you reach the next restaurant, unless you curtail all stops. The park is located along the Cabot Trail, named

149

for explorer John Cabot, who sailed into Aspy Bay, near Dingwall, in 1497, only five years after Christopher Columbus visited the Caribbean. Soon after Cabot's discovery of this neck of the woods, European fishermen and fur traders began visiting these shores, eager to make their fortunes from the natural bounty of the area.

The main interpretive center is at the park entrance. In the same building is a bookstore. Apart from the maps and information for sale or offered there, you'll have a chance to explore what has to be the most extensive collection of naturalist books you may ever see.

The park is full of natural wonders, from huge, 300-year-old sugar maples, yellow birch, and beech trees, to waterfalls rushing down rugged mountainsides, to eagles soaring gracefully in their wilderness refuge, to the black bear, which will tolerate no insult from human intruders who roam the park's interior. Take heed and photograph any bears that you may happen to spot with a telephoto lens. You may see a moose along the road in the park, so drive cautiously.

The park has been carefully mapped out with twenty-eight suggested trails, some challenging overnight ones, and some just twenty minutes long and on level ground. There are also plenty of places to stop and park your car for panoramic views of the ocean or river rapids far below the road which winds its way around the highlands. Pick up a detailed map at the park entrance as well as the booklet entitled "Walking in the Highlands," which outlines the many hikes and has them conveniently arranged with numbers corresponding to indicators on the map.

Soon after you've entered the parkland itself, you will come to an area inhabited at one time by French Acadians. Several trails along the Chéticamp River are reminders of this area's first European settlers. If the long hike to **Pleasant Bay** is not your style, you can still get excellent views of the coastline from several lookoff points along this part of the route.

On a very clear day it is worthwhile to make a stop at the **Fishing Cove Lookoff.** Cast your gaze northwest into the St. Lawrence. The islands you will see are 50 miles (80 km) away: Quebec's Magdalene Islands. (They are sufficiently close that you will have seen a sign for a Magdalene Islands ferry in Chéticamp. Locals, however, say that lack of interest keeps the ferry from sailing regularly.)

Try to imagine the intense isolation of this area of Cape Breton in the 1920s. The ice forms for miles out to sea in the winter. Before the minister of highways of the time conceived of the idea of building the road from Chéticamp to Pleasant Bay and beyond, and then turning the area into parkland, it was virtually impossible to make one's way beyond the next farmhouse during the many winter storms.

From the park entrance to Pleasant Bay takes about an hour by car if you stop only a few times to look around. This little village is just on the outside of the national park, since the highway meanders outside park boundaries temporarily. During the summer months you may be able to dine at one of the few motels that operate here and also run small restaurants.

Just north of Pleasant Bay, in the direction of Red River, a **Buddhist monastery** has been established, after its founder, a Tibetan lama, found the environment suitable for contemplation. Once you've roamed around the Cape Breton Highlands for a while, you'll understand why.

When you exit Pleasant Bay along the Cabot Trail you will return to official national park territory within a few minutes. You will then steadily climb uphill while making a number of turns. Be on the lookout for a sign that indicates the **Lone Shieling** and parking. If you don't grab a chance to park at this spot, it will be too late to look at the Lone Shieling itself except for a perfunctory glance as you whiz past in your automobile.

Once you do park you have before you one of the most pleasant and interesting short walks that the park has to offer. The loop takes about a quarter hour, if you don't count the time you spend at the replica of a Scottish crofter's hut. The building was erected at the request of a man named Donald MacIntosh, a native of Pleasant Bay and a professor of geology at Dalhousie University. He donated one hundred acres (40 hectares) to the government in the area of Pleasant Bay in 1934, including some virgin forest. (The park has 80 percent of the province's remaining virgin forest.) After the land was absorbed into the budding national park, the government built this replica of the Lone Shieling, a crofter's hut like those on the Isle of Skye, from whence this man's family came. It's a cleverly constructed little shelter; one can well imagine a shepherd huddled in here with his sheep when storms made the out-of-doors unpleasant.

Lone Shieling on the Cabot Trail

After viewing the hut descend a small set of stairs and walk along a woodland path in an area of tall, ancient yellow birch and 350-year-old sugar maple trees, accompanied by interpretive park signs. The trail ends with another set of stone steps leading up to the parking area.

Another few minutes' driving time from here will take you high up into the mountains, to a point where scenic views are around every corner. The best panoramic shots are cleverly desig-nated by small lookout symbols and a widening of the road that permits parking. From one of these lookouts (indicated on the park map), you can see in the distance the **Beulach Ban Falls,** which can also be reached by a trail at the base of the mountain.

To get to the falls, follow the directions to a trail called the **Aspy,** the entrance to which begins at a turnoff just after the warden station. Take note that while the first part is accessible by vehicle, the road requires a high wheelbase and good suspension in the spring.

Then, once again, the road exits official park territory and leads through a stretch of rural Cape Breton where you won't have an opportunity to eat for miles and miles, until at long last you come to **Cape North** and **Dingwall.** Here, finally, the hungry traveler can find several promising spots, starting with **Morrison's Pioneer Restaurant,** in Cape North. This restaurant has the look and feel of a rural museum or antiques shop, decorated as it is with the authentic memorabilia of the area's early Scottish settlers. Entrees cost roughly $10, and the menu is standard fare for tourist eateries—pasta, salmon, and chowder, and other seafood offerings.

At Cape North the road forks, with the left turn leading to the pretty coastal communities of **Bay St. Lawrence, Capstick,** and **Meat Cove.** Then the road stops. If you want to see more of the rugged coast, you can take a whale-watching cruise aboard a Cape Islander boat owned by **Captain Dennis Cox** in Capstick. He can be reached by calling (902) 383–2981. In addition to the frequent sightings of whales on this cruise, you'll stand a good chance of seeing eagles, cormorants, lots of puffins, moose, bear, waterfalls, and sea caves.

After experiencing Capstick you have no choice but to turn your car south from whence you came and return to the fork in the road at Cape North. (Take note that on a really foggy day, you may as well pass up this detour altogether, because you'll hardly be able to see anything.) If you take the right instead of the left road, and then drive for a moment, you will come to the turnoff for Dingwall, which is precisely 2 miles (3 km) after Cape North.

This road will take you to **The Markland Resort** in Dingwall. The Markland is considered by some to be the rival of the Keltic Lodge, which is a posh government-run resort in Ingonish. The Markland features rustic, Scandinavian-style pine chalets spread out over 70 acres (28 hectares) overlooking the ocean. A long, secluded, sandy beach here is complemented by a stretch of inland waterway suitable for water sports. For details call (902) 383–2246. Rates are moderate.

During the summer months the Markland also operates a gourmet restaurant; this is virtually your last chance to eat until you get to Ingonish. The restaurant is open only from late June to mid-October.

There are two options for heading southeast out of Cape North: You can drive through official park territory, or take the scenic route along a coastal road from **Effies Brook** to **New Haven.** Although the scenic route takes a bit longer, it's well worth it. There is a potential picture postcard around every bend.

This loop ends at the tiny community of **Neil's Harbour,** which has a lighthouse and a picnic area where you can stretch your legs and roam around amid fishing shacks and lobster traps. Then it's back into the park for another stretch of hilly driving, until you reach **Ingonish,** and then **Middle Head,** which is lumped in with Ingonish whenever anyone talks about it as a destination.

Middle Head is the site of ◆ **Keltic Lodge,** not Ingonish, as you might hear. Keltic is the granddaddy of all Cape Breton resorts, perched majestically on a high promontory overlooking Ingonish Beach. Even if you don't stay here, it is worth your while to roam the grounds and enjoy the setting and view before moving on down the trail.

While Keltic Lodge is in a lovely setting, and takes a fabulous picture, expect to pay roughly 50 percent more for accommodations here than at the Markland for the same number of rating stars. The restaurant at Keltic, the posh **Atlantic Restaurant,** is probably the only one on the island that requires that male patrons wear a jacket to dinner. But Keltic is adjacent to an eighteen-hole golf course and is close enough to skiing hills that special packages are available for the ski season. To one side of Ingonish Beach is a freshwater lake with supervised swimming. You can reach Keltic by calling (800) 565-0444. Rates are deluxe.

Continuing along the Cabot Trail in the Ingonish area, you will soon see a sign on the right for ◆ **Lynn Gorey's Craft Shop and Art Gallery.** This is a must-see. "Lynn" is the wife of widely acclaimed artist Christopher Gorey, whose work is displayed in this shop (as well as at the Nova Scotia Art Gallery in Halifax).

Along with wonderful, full-size original watercolors, which can be had for a few hundred dollars, Gorey has limited-edition reproductions in sizes that pack easily, unframed, for only $20 and up.

Gorey, whose studio is located in the back of the art gallery, depicts life on this coast with a special sensitivity for his medium.

From Ingonish you'll return ever so briefly to the national park, to climb one last mountain along a winding road. This is where the advice to travel the trail clockwise from Chéticamp to Ingonish comes in handy: If you went in the other direction, you would be "cliffside" on the road.

Die-hard cyclists love to "do" the Cabot Trail; often you will see one plodding away in his or her lowest gear up **Cape Smokey.** If this is the case, exercise extreme caution, because cyclists often need considerable leeway on the road and cannot stop safely. (My husband has cycled the trail five times, and he assures me that brakes won't work on the descent, even if you want to use them.)

A pleasant stretch of coastal road awaits you after leaving the national park for good. This area is sometimes referred to as **St. Ann's Loop.** Here there is an eclectic mix of artists and craftspeople who have been drawn to the area by its bucolic charm.

In **Indian Brook** you'll notice a rustic wooden home and shop called **Leather Works,** on the right-hand side of the road. Operated by John Roberts, the store features historic reproductions of traditional leather goods, including leather buckets, which modern-day owners use to chill champagne or as elegant flower pots. Leather buckets are lighter than wooden ones, so back in the days when brigades of men passed water buckets hand over hand, these were the type used. Pitch was used to water-seal them.

The owner of Leather Works, a former Ontario resident, specializes in leather reproductions for national parks and museums across the country. When you visit the Fortress Louisbourg, for example, farther along in Cape Breton, take note of the fire brigade's leather buckets. These were reproductions made by Roberts.

Along with the buckets, and belts, purses, and shoes at Leather Works, you will find tavern-style aprons in supple leather that are *très chic.*

A few moments' drive after Indian Brook will bring you to a tiny ferry crossing at **Jersey Cove.** Here you have the option of continuing to drive to South Gut St. Ann's at the head of St. Ann's Harbour, or taking a 50-cent car ferry ride across the narrow harbor. The ferry is a good bet, and an unbeatable bargain.

BRAS D'OR LAKE REGION

On the other side of the harbor is **Englishtown,** which has the distinction of being the birthplace and final resting place of a famous Cape Breton giant and one-time P. T. Barnum circus performer, Angus MacAskill. Just a minute after you drive off the boat, you will spot a small graveyard where the 7-foot-9-inch (2.4-m), 425-pound (193-kg) giant is buried. Not surprisingly, his is the biggest headstone.

Five minutes' drive farther down Route 312 will bring you to the ✦ **Giant MacAskill Museum,** which contains all sorts of memorabilia. A sign indicates the museum on Route 312.

Open from Victoria Day (usually the third Monday in May) to Thanksgiving (the second Monday in October), the house contains artifacts—big ones, like massive boots and the giant's chair. These items from MacAskill's life and times provide a fascinating picture of one of the most unusual people of his day. A full-scale model of the giant (at one time displayed at the Halifax Citadel) gives you a good idea of the commanding presence of the man. For information call (902) 929–2106.

From here the drive to **South Gut St. Ann's** is quite straight-forward. Route 312 ends momentarily at Junction 12, where you will join TransCanada Highway 105, headed south. Follow this route for 3.5 miles (5 km) until you reach Exit 11. If you take this exit, you will find yourself in front of the ✦ **Lobster Galley at Harbour House.**

Complete with its own lobster pound at the inner limit of St. Ann's Harbour, you can guess what the specialty is at the restaurant. (A waitress here, however, noted that they also serve vegetarian and macrobiotic items, and she estimated that one eighth of their customers request vegetarian fare. Word of mouth has been sufficient to bring in large groups of Buddhist monks on the way to the abbey in Pleasant Bay.)

The Harbour House also has a gift shop. A nice touch on the menu is the "Gaelic Language Primer," complete with pronunciations. The English translations alone sound typical of Gaelic speakers, since they use colloquialisms and a sentence structure not wholly English.

Gaelic has only eighteen letters in its alphabet, but it has sounds unheard of in English due to the unusual combination of letters. Here are a few essentials:

Ciamar a tha thu-fhein, pronounced "Kimmer uh ha oo haen?" meaning, "How's yourself?" (It's their translation, not mine.)

De do naigheachd, pronounced "Jae daw neh ochk?" meaning "What's new?"

Se biadh math a bha sin, pronounced "Sheh bee ugh ma uh va shin," meaning, "That was a lovely meal."

Am feum mi na soithichean a nighe? pronounced "Um faem nuh seh eechyun uh nee uh?," and meaning, "Must I wash the dishes?"

Right next door is the ✦ **Gaelic College of Celtic Arts and Crafts,** where no doubt the students can make sense of the primer. Locally known as **St. Anne's Gaelic College,** it is a place where visitors can explore the legacy of Scottish settlers to North America at the "Great Hall of the Clans." There is also a museum and craft shop. For information call (902) 295–3411.

Now the center of Gaelic education on the island and, in fact, host to visiting students from the Old World, St. Ann's has an interesting story attached to it. In the last century a group of 800 Scottish settlers decided that life in Cape Breton was just too hard, the soil too unyielding, the winters too long. Led by a Presbyterian minister, they pulled up stakes and moved to New Zealand. Today thousands of New Zealanders can trace their roots to a one-time Scottish settler in this area of Nova Scotia.

Who could have predicted that a century after the Scottish settlers had abandoned their homes in St. Ann's that the village would be the center of Scottish revivalism? One thing is certain: The story of the exodus to New Zealand does not get much play at the Gaelic College.

The first Scottish attempt at settling Cape Breton was in 1629, when a baronet named Lord Ochiltree promoted Cape Breton and its qualities. The King had established an order of baronets five years earlier, who were to promote and oversee the settlement of tracts of land 3 by 6 miles (5 by 10 km) along the coast. The rough equivalent of modern-day real estate developers, these baronets were gambling not just their personal fortunes but their lives.

Soon after Lord Ochiltree landed at Baliene, on the island's east coast, he discovered French fishing vessels in what was supposed to be British waters. The baronet sent a ship to tell them they could stay to fish and trade with the Micmac if they paid him 10 percent of their earnings. They then took the first mate hostage and kept three cannon as collateral until the French captain was able to pay.

At about this time yet another declaration of peace was being signed between France and England. Meanwhile, another sea captain named Daniels arrived from France, landing at St. Ann's, where some French settlers told him about the Scottish pioneers at Baliene. Peace declarations aside, Captain Daniels determined to teach Ochiltree a lesson, gathered together his hardiest men, had scaling ladders constructed, and went to make a neighborly call on Ochiltree. Once inside Scottish walls, Daniels captured Ochiltree. His men subdued the baronet's armor-clad soldiers. Once again a French flag flew over the island. Baronet Ochiltree was taken prisoner along with all his men and brought to St. Ann's, where the most able Scotsmen among them were set to work building the French a fort, chapel, and magazine. By November 1629, Captain Daniels sailed for France with his captives, a number of whom died en route and were thrown overboard. Our hapless land speculator ended up in France, where he made unheeded appeals to the Court of Admiralty in Dieppe. Finally, Captain Daniels sailed off on another adventure, and Nova Scotia's unfortunate baronet was released. The entire misadventure had cost him £50,000 and thirteen men.

From St. Ann's drive south back along the same stretch of highway and you will once again reach Exit 11, which brings you to the TransCanada. Follow it south until Exit 10, which is the junction leading to **Baddeck,** your next destination, and the perfect spot for exploring the beauty of the **Bras d'Or Lake.**

Nova Scotia is home to one of the highest concentrations of ❖ **bald eagles** in North America. There are an estimated 250 nesting pairs of eagles, found for the most part along the shores of the Bras d'Or Lake. Incidentally, this isn't really a lake at all, but an inland sea with mildly salty water, at 5 percent salt content, sufficient to keep a lobster fishery going. Its total area is 450 square miles (1,165 sq. km).

Because it has virtually no tide, the saltwater arm of the sea freezes solid in winter. During July and August you'll have ample opportunity to see the eagles in their native environment. The birds are sufficiently plentiful and healthy that some newborn eagles are now being exported to the United States, especially to the Quabbin Reservoir area of central Massachusetts.

Reproduction problems were experienced by many birds in the 1960s, due to DDT and other chemical insecticides in the food chain. In the isolation of the Nova Scotia coastline, these problems did not arise, leaving the province with healthy communities of raptors, including ospreys, hawks, and owls.

Several suggested routes to take to get a better look at the eagles include Highway 223, through the central Bras d'Or Lake district, and TransCanada Highway 105, which skirts the northern outer rim of Bras d'Or. Pay particular attention to the "Scenic Travelways Map," available at all of the province's tourism information booths. Along the map's outline of the lake are logos of bald eagles, marking the best places for viewing them.

Several sailing tours are available in the area, since the lake is a haven for sailors. (Boats can get in from the northern inlet that you recently crossed by ferry, or through the St. Peter's Canal, at the southern tip of Cape Breton. If it were not for a short strip of land now traversed by the St. Peter's Canal, Cape Breton would really be two islands, not one.)

Try ✦**Amoeba's Sailing Tours,** which operate out of Baddeck. Amoeba's has a schooner that promises not only a good look at eagles in their natural setting but also a view of telephone inventor Alexander Graham Bell's stately mansion. Reservations are a good idea. Fares for Amoeba's Sailing Tours are $16.00 for adults, $14.00 for seniors, and $8.00 for chidren ages ten to sixteen. Children under ten go free. Call (902) 295–2481 or (902) 295–1426.

Helen Sievers, the owner of ✦ **Gisele's Country Inn** in Baddeck, capitalizes on the beautiful natural setting of the village by arranging a number of outings for her guests, including searches for wild mushrooms and other edible wild plants. Sievers uses as her guide a local naturalist. She says that one year they even managed to find truffles, which they froze and kept on hand for cooking at the inn's four-star restaurant. Another favorite is fiddleheads, (at their peak in May).

Gisele's has a long, sweeping lawn built up a hill, giving such a picturesque view of Baddeck that painters sometimes set up an easel there. Gisele's can be reached by calling (902) 295–2849 or fax (902) 295–2033. Rates are moderate.

Also in the Baddeck area you can visit the **Alexander Graham Bell Museum and National Historic Site.** Bell spent his summers here for many years, and spent quite a bit of time here in the winter as well. Displays on his many inventions tell his life story.

Bell was initially involved in speech therapy, as were his father and grandfather. His mother was partially deaf, and Bell eventually married one of his deaf students. His work on the telephone came as a result of his intense interest in communications technology. Along with inventing the phone at age twenty-nine, he worked on airplane development, building the *Silver Dart,* which was flown over Bras d'Or Lake (he used the frozen lake as his tarmac for take-off and landing). He also built a hydrofoil, the original HD-40 version of which is on display at the museum. Of course, you also get to see lots of early telephones. Admission is $2.50. It is open year-round from 9:00 A.M. to 5:00 P.M., with the hours extended to 8:00 P.M. in July and August and to 6:00 P.M. in September.

Baddeck is an anomaly: This tiny village with a population of slightly more than 1,000 souls swells to several times this number in the summer without being frazzled. The result is a collection of good eateries along the waterfront and a number of interesting things to do. The community even has a ferry that takes people over to nearby **Kidston Island's beach** for free.

The **Bell Buoy** provides scrumptuous desserts, delicious seafood, and a great view of the lake, including the little lighthouse on Kidston Island, which is just facing the restaurant. You'll also see a lot of yachts. Since it's a charming little community with a good marina, it has become a haunt of yachters who love the Bras d'Or for its excellent sailing.

Bell's stately summer home overlooks the inlet where the village is nestled, just across from a small island and lighthouse. The home's setting couldn't be prettier.

Another cozy restaurant operates out of the ◆ **Telegraph House,** which has been an inn for more than a century. In the late 1880s it was the home-away-from-home of Alexander Graham Bell before his mansion was built on the stretch of headland overlooking the lake. The building also housed the telegraph office at one time. Today it is owned and operated by the fourth and fifth generations of the Dunlop family. Room number one, Bell's room, has been left in very much the same state as when he used it.

The Victorian home was built in 1861 and has hosted dinner for Prince Michael, brother of the Duke of Kent, and a Prince and Princess of Japan, photographs of whom are displayed at the inn.

The place is utterly charming, right down to the fireside armchairs and grandfather clock. For information call (902) 295–9988.

Moving from the Baddeck area into the forest hinterland, you can take the time for one of the most scenic walks in this end of the country, culminating at the ✦ **Uisage Bann Falls,** Gaelic for "white water." To get there you will have to backtrack about 1 mile (1.6 km) to the Cabot Trail (which terminates at Baddeck) on Route 105, just after the TransCanada junction leading to Baddeck. A sign indicating a left turnoff will direct you to the falls. Follow the signs to a parking lot, where you can leave your vehicle and proceed on foot up a moderately steep incline for about 1 mile (1.6 km), past a stream that runs through a thick stand of birch and evergreens. At the end your reward will be the sort of astoundingly beautiful, ice-cold waterfall that could have been used in a Robin Hood movie.

Once you're on the road again and have left Baddeck behind, turn southward, on Route 105, in the direction of **Little Narrows.** From here you can take another little ferry across a narrow arm of the lake onto a small patch of land, the **Washabuck Peninsula,** which is practically an island itself.

You will have a choice of two directions as soon as you get off the ferry. Choose the road to your right, the southern end of Route 223. This road will take you through rolling hills that yield a beautiful view of the lake, an area that seems completely untouched by the modern world. As such, it is a likely setting for the ✦ **Highland Village,** in **Iona,** just before the recently built bridge that spans the Barra Strait.

Just before you approach the new bridge, turn right and follow the shore road a short way. High on a hilltop overlooking the Bras d'Or, you will find a replica of an old Scottish pioneer village. There are homes from 1830, 1865, and 1900, as well as a thatch-roof Hebridean Black house of the type used by the earliest settlers and a log house. There are also a school, forge, carding mill, and barn. Costumed guides will show you around. On the first Saturday in August each year they hold Highland Village Day, with traditional Scottish music. Admission is $4.00 for adults. Students to grade six pay 50 cents, grades seven to twelve pay $1.00. Families pay $8.00; seniors pay $3.00. Phone is (902) 725–2272.

From Iona drive across the bridge to **Grand Narrows.** This is a wonderful, unspoiled spot worth spending some time at. There is good swimming, with warm water, at **Piper's Cove,** just after Grand Narrows. You can also **charter a boat** from Elaine and

Terry MacNeil, phone (902) 622–2743, that will take you all around this end of the lake, including as far south as the Crammond Islands for mussels. The rate is $60 an hour for the boatload.

You can take either Route 223, along St. Andrew's Channel on the northern end of this peninsula, or the southern route, past Eskasoni, a large Micmac community. Regardless of which end of highway you choose, head to Sydney so that you do not find yourself trying to get to Louisbourg on secondary roads with rough patches.

Sydney, population 26,000, is a good spot for a rest stop. There are a number of interesting things to see here. You will enter the city on Route 4, which quickly becomes King's Road until you reach the city core. This is a city built by the coal and steel industries of the past century. These days there is a small university here and the city serves as a service hub for the island.

A number of historic buildings can be found here. ◆ **Cossit House,** reputed to be the oldest building in Sydney, dates back to 1787. You will find it at 75 Charlotte Street. It's part of the Nova Scotia Museum Complex. Carefully restored to its original condition, it includes furnishings listed in an inventory of the building in 1815. Cossit House was the home of the island's first Anglican minister.

To get to Cossit House, continue along King's Road until it becomes the Esplanade. This ends at the corner of Prince Street, which is also, mysteriously, named Route 4. Follow the waterfront for 4 more blocks and then turn right onto Charlotte Street.

Cossit House is 1 block away from the river. Apart from the costumed guides and antiques, it has a pretty garden. It is open only from June 1 to October 15, from 9:30 A.M. to 5:30 P.M. For more information call (902) 539–7973.

Also on Charlotte Street, and just a stone's throw away at number 54, is ◆ **Jost House.** It gives one a good idea of how homes evolved on Cape Breton over the years, including artifacts related to old-style cooking and baking. Jost House is open year-round from 10:00 A.M. to 4:00 P.M. daily, except in the winter, when it opens Sunday at 1:00 P.M. and closes on Monday. For information call (902) 539–0366.

One other particularly noteworthy historic house is now a country inn, with a renowned restaurant. **The Gowrie House,** at 139 Shore Road in Sydney Mines, is a 3½-star establishment set in a home dating back to 1834. To visit, you'll have to detour across the harbor to Highway 223 northbound, to Sydney Mines.

THE FLEUR-DE-LIS TRAIL

Once you've seen enough of Sydney, take Highway 22, which runs straight off George Street downtown. Highway 22 is the most direct route to take to see The Fortress Louisbourg, North America's largest and most authentic historical restoration, but there are many other routes.

Highway 22 takes you across the **Mira River,** which has been immortalized by one of Cape Breton's most popular ballads. (If you're in the Maritimes for any length of time, you're bound to hear "Song for the Mira.") Just after crossing the Mira, you will reach a community called Albert Bridge, where on the left-hand side of the road is an excellent craft shop and gallery, which no doubt owes its existence to its location in such a beautiful setting. Called the ◆**Old Mira Trading Post,** the shop carries Micmac crafts, along with antiques and other craft items like handknit sweaters and quilts. It publicizes its "top rate on American money," so if you are traveling from the United States, you might keep it in mind.

Just 2 miles (3 km) east off Route 22 at Exit 17 in **Albert Bridge,** you will find the **Mira River Provincial Park,** where there are facilities for swimming and picnicking. Because the land at this part of the river forms a peninsula, there are several little coves and secluded swimming areas as well as launch sites for canoes. Along this river, and in **Catalone,** just 2 miles (3 km) farther along Route 22, many locals have summer cottages.

Back on Route 22, just before you reach Louisbourg, you will come to the old ◆**Sydney and Louisbourg Railway Station Museum.** It features two wonderful, full-sized, turn-of-the-century railway coach cars in mint condition, a caboose, an oil car, and a freight car—sufficient paraphernalia to satisfy any railway buff. The museum also chronicles the salad days of Louisbourg, when shipping, mining, and the railway made this excellent harbor a thriving community. The building that houses what is left of the railway is the station, which, along with the freight shed, was constructed in 1895, an era when this little stretch of rail had more than 4 million tons of coal a year hauled across its ribbon of steel.

163

Sadly, the original roundhouse is gone. But an exact replica has been constructed and is used to house the rolling stock during the winter months. For more details on the local area, the railway museum also houses an information center.

Along with railway memorabilia the museum has many photographs chronicling the three transatlantic Marconi wireless stations established by Italian inventor Guglielmo Marconi. At the turn of the century, Marconi spent several years near Glace Bay in Cape Breton, establishing his wireless stations.

Just after the railway museum, you'll arrive in **Louisbourg,** the tiny downtown area of which seems to be thriving with businesses catering to summer visitors to the ◆ **Fortress Louisbourg.**

It's an amazing turn of events, when you consider what an unfortunate location the original fortress had. It lay on windswept land, surrounded by hills that left it quite exposed to attacks, so barren that it was difficult to cultivate food for the fortress's inhabitants. It was located here because the magnificent harbor had been discovered by Europeans by 1713, leading to the founding of a town. It soon became the East Coast's third-busiest seaport. Because it was far closer to France than the scattered settlements along the St. Lawrence, no price seemed too high to pay in the defense of the "Gibraltar of the North."

The restoration has been arranged to re-create life in the town during a summer's day in 1744, the peak of French power in the New World. Along with a garrison of 600 soldiers was a permanent population of approximately 2,000 administrators, clerks, innkeepers, cooks, artisans, and fishermen. The restored fortress includes fifty buildings, (one quarter of the original town). Local residents, many descended from the original French settlers, portray the residents of the French garrison town.

When you arrive at the fortress gate, you are immediately accosted by a French "soldier," who demands to know your business there. One hundred interpreters in full costume explain intricate details of life at Louisbourg in 1744.

In the chapel, actually an impressive church that is part of the fortifications, tiny model ships hang in the window. These traditionally were built by fishermen as a way of expressing their gratitude to God for a good catch. Only the elite sat in the church; all others stood, so it held hundreds at a single mass.

The governor's wheelchair in his chambers dates from that era. His room is adorned with carefully reproduced portraits and period furniture.

Take note of the open fireplaces where meat was roasted on spits. Cooks would turn a mechanical device, which in turn would evenly rotate the spit, untended for a half hour or so before the cook had to attend to the basting.

Ultimately, the location that made winters severe and cultivation difficult also led to the downfall of the fortress. In 1745, one year after the summer's day you see re-enacted, an expedition of New England volunteers laid siege to Louisbourg's barely complete defenses. The fortress garrison held out for several weeks.

During the following winter, 900 of the victorious New Englanders died of cold and starvation. The dead had to be buried under floorboards until spring.

Finally, the New England soldiers mutinied and drowned their sorrows in drink. When reinforcements arrived, the new British governor ordered their rum confiscated. A total of 64,000 gallons was seized.

Three years later, Louisbourg was briefly returned to the French. In 1758, a year before the fall of Quebec, a force of 15,000 British soldiers and more than 150 ships attacked, blowing the fortress to smithereens.

For years afterward Louisbourg was nothing more than a source of cut stone and hardware for buildings even as far away as the newly founded Halifax. Eventually, because it did not have a modern city constructed over it, the ruins allowed for an amazingly authentic restoration.

A modest admission fee is charged. Adults pay $7.50, seniors pay $6.00, students and children pay $4.25, and a family rate is $19.25 to tour the site. For more information call (902) 733–2280.

After Louisbourg you have very little option but to return almost to Sydney on Highway 22, then exit to Highway 4 southbound, just outside the city. From here you will skirt the southern end of the Bras D'Or Lake until you reach **St. Peter's.**

If you happen to be in Cape Breton near the end of July, you are a lucky visitor indeed, because then you can take in ◆ **The Big Pond Festival,** held every year in **Big Pond,** which you will pass through en route to St. Peter's. This is an excellent musical showcase of East Coast talent, featuring Big Pond's own Rita Mac-Neil, who is now an international recording artist.

The reward of this slight backtracking to Highway 4 will be self-evident: The road passes through breathtaking scenery, particularly late in the day as the sun sets over the lake.

In St. Peter's the land narrows so much that, for want of a few inches of water, Cape Breton would consist of two major islands instead of one. One hundred and forty years ago, the opportunities presented by this geographic fact led to the building of the **St. Peter's Canal.** Before that time, the area was the haunt of French fur trader and adventurer Nicolas Denys, who eventually became the governor of New France in the late 1600s.

Everything there is to see in St. Peter's is within walking distance of the rustic log structure of the charming **Bras D'Or Lakes Inn,** which fronts on the lake. If you stay at the inn, take note of the log-construction hardwood chairs and furnishings. These were made by a local furniture artisan.

A short walk from the inn will take you to the canal, along which you can walk for a considerable distance. On the north side you will find **Battery Park,** a pleasant place where you can stroll around the point of land or turn southward and cross the canal along walkways that form the top of the locks.

Between the lake and the ocean there is a differential of 8 inches (20 cm) of water, between high and low tides. Because of the calm seas, it is a haven for pleasure boaters, many of whom use the canal to enter the Bras D'Or.

On a hill overlooking the south side of the canal is the **Nicolas Denys Museum.** The building is a modern reconstruction of an old-style French fur-trading post, of the sort historians think was used at the time of Denys' stay in Cape Breton. In the 1650s, shortly after his time in Miscou and before he decamped to Bathurst, Denys had a post here. It's a small museum, but it does recount the life of one of the most exciting and adventurous explorers of the French colonial era. It is open from June 1 to the end of September. There is an admission fee of 50 cents for adults and 25 cents for children. For more information call (902) 535–2379.

Another worthwhile stop in St. Peter's is a short walk from the canal. Situated on Main Street (Highway 4) is a small, unassuming, 115-year-old house, the birthplace of one of the country's most famous photographers. The ❧ **Wallace MacAskill Museum** contains twenty-six of the marine photographer's hand-tinted photographs as well as biographical material.

MacAskill was the photographer who literally made **Peggy's Cove** into the tourist icon it has become. His photographs from the 1930s, when it was depicted as the ultimate sleepy little fishing village, set the stage for the growth of the tourist industry in this province. His most famous photograph is accessible to millions: Just reach into your pocket and pull out a Canadian dime.

That's a MacAskill, of the original *Bluenose*.

With St. Peter's your tour of Cape Breton is almost complete, except for a stop at the ❧ **LeNoir Forge Museum on Isle Madame.** Leaving St. Peter's, you can continue along Highway 4 or take Provincial Highway 104. Either way, to visit Isle Madame you will have to turn off at Exit 46, near Louisdale, and drive to **Arichat.** Here again you will find an Acadian community, many of whom are descendants of exiled Acadians who returned to these shores.

Added to this mix, you will again find the trail of Jersey Island money and investors in the fishing industry who moved into the area as soon as the land was ceded to England. Arichat may seem like a sleepy little village now, but 200 years ago it was one of the continent's biggest fishing boomtowns. In the 1700s, at the height of this fish-based economic boom, a stone blacksmith was set up right along the shoreline for the purpose of forging whatever tools were needed. You will find this impressive restored stone smithy harborside, just 1 block off Route 320 in Arichat. Admission is free, but it is frequently closed when it ought to be open, so call ahead to confirm times if your sole purpose in visiting Arichat is to see the blacksmith shop. The phone number is (902) 226–9364.

If you have visited Isle Madame, you will need to return to Exit 46 via either Highway 206 or 320. From Exit 46 southbound you can take either Provincial Highway 104 or the slightly more scenic Highway 4, to Port Hastings, the Canso Causeway, and beyond, bringing to a close your tour of Cape Breton.

INDEX

Acadian Cemetery, 111
Acadian Historical Village,
  N.B., 33
Albert Bridge, 163
Alberton, 53
Alexander Graham Bell
  Museum and National His-
  toric Site, 159
Amoeba's Sailing Tours, 159
Anchorage Provincial Park, 11
Andrew's Mist, The, 53
An Drochaid, 139
Angus MacAskill, 156
Annapolis Royal, 118–22
Annapolis Royal Historic Gar-
  dens, 121
Anne of Green Gables
  Museum at Silver Bush, 58
Antique Automobile Museum,
  25
Antonine Maillet, 37
Apple Blossom Festival, 131
Arichat, 167
Aristotle's Lantern, 9
Arrowhead Lodge, 67
Artists' Workshop, 10
Atlantic Restaurant, 154
Atlantic Wind Test Site, 51

Baddeck, 158
Baie des Chaleurs, 30, 34
Balancing Rock, 114
Barrington Woolen Mill, 99
Basin Head, 69

Basin Head Fisheries Museum,
  69
Bass River, 132
Bathurst, 32
Battery Park, 166
Bayberry Cliff Inn, 74
Beaconsfield Historic House,
  62
Beaver River, 108
Beaverbrook Art Gallery, 15
Beausejour, 38
Bell Buoy, 160
Belliveau Cove, 111
Belliveau Cove Wharf, 112
Beulach Ban Falls, 152
Big and Little Tancook Islands,
  83
Big Pond Festival, 165
Birchtown, 97
Birdland, 80
Bishop MacEachern National
  Historic Site, 64
Blue Heron Pottery, 59
Bohaker Trail, 124
Borden, 44
Boscawen Inn, 87
Bouctouche, 37
Bras d'Or Lake, 158–59, 166
Bras D'Or Lakes Inn, 166
Brier Island Lodge, 115
Brier Island, 114
Brudenell, 71
Brudenell River Provincial
  Park, 71

Buffaloland Provincial Park, 72

Cabot Beach Provincial Park, 58
Cabot Trail, 144–55
Campbellton, 28–30
Campobello Island, 6–7
Campobello Island's Roosevelt Cottage, 7–8
Cape Blomidon, 130
Cape Breton Highlands National Park, 149
Cap–Egmont Bottle Houses, 48–9
Cape Fourchu, 104
Cape North, 153
Cape Smokey, 155
Cape Split, 129
Cape St. Mary's, 110
Cape View Diner, 110
Cap Pelé Beach, 37
Capstick, 153
Captain Garry's Seal and Bird Watching Cruises, 74
Captain's House Inn, 84
Caraquet, 34
Carleton Martello Tower, 12–13
Carriage House Inn, 17
Castalia, 11
Cavendish, 59
Cedar Bog, 50
Cedar Dunes Provincial Park, 48
Ceilidh at the Irish Hall, 63
Centre Plein Air du Vieux Moulin, 26

Chaleur Phantom, 30
Changing of the Guard, 14
Charlie's Trail, 124
Charlottetown, 44
Charlottetown, 62–64
Chester, 84–85
Chester Playhouse, 85
Chéticamp, 145–49
Chéticamp Island, 148
Chez La Vigne, 131
Christ Church Cathedral, 16
Churchill Mansion, 108
Church Point, 110
Citadel, 80
Clark's Harbour, Cape Sable Island, 100
Claude Chaloux, 111
Cold Comfort Farm, 53
Compass Rose, 9
Concession, 111
Confederation Centre of the Arts, 64
Confederation Trail, 53, 67–68
Coopérative Artisanale de Chéticamp Ltée, 146
Cooper's Inn, 96
Coquillages & Couleurs/Galerie Boutique, 112
Cossit House, 162
Covered Bridge Number Four, 6
Crab'n 'Apple Bed and Breakfast, 66
Crêpes Bretonne Restaurant, 34
Crescent Beach, 94

Cruise Manada, 72
Cultural Pioneer Village, 47

Dalvay-by-the-Sea, 61
Daly Point Reserve, 32
Deer Island, 6
Deer Island Point Park, 6
Delap's Cove, 123–24
Demonstration woodlot, 69
Digby Neck, 114
Dock Street, 98
Doctor's Inn Organic Market
    and Garden, 55
Dory Shop, 98
Duck Pond Inn, 108
Dufferin Inn and San Martello
    Dining Room, 12
Duncreigan Inn, 140
Dunes Studio Gallery, 61

East Point Lighthouse, 67
Edmundston, 24
Eel River Sandbar, 31
Église Ste.-Marie, 110
Elephant Rock, 51
Elmira, 67
Elmira Railway Museum,
    67–68
Englishtown, 156
Étoile de Mer, 47

Fenderson Beach at Jacquet
    River Park, 31
Firefighters Museum, 102
Fisheries Museum of the
    Atlantic, 87
Five Islands Provincial Park, 133

Fixed Link, 38, 44
Forestry Museum, 27
Fort Anne, 118, 120
Fortress Louisbourg, 164–65
Fredericton, 14
Freeman's Pharmacy, 143
French Village (PEI), 59
French Village (NS), 82
Fundy Geological Museum, 134
Fundy National Park, 39

Gaelic College of Celtic Arts
    and Crafts, 157
Gallery of Roger Savage, 91
Giant MacAskill Museum, 156
Gilbert Cove, 114
Gisele's Country Inn, 159
Glencoe Mills Hall, 142
Glenora Falls, 142
Glooscap Trail, 131–35
Gowrie House, 162–63
Grand Falls, 22
Grand Manan Island, 8–12
Grand Narrows, 161
Granny's Trunk, 60
Granville Ferry, 121
Grosses Coques, 111

Habitation, 121–23
Halifax, 79–82
Harbour Restaurant, 147
Hartland, 19
Harvest Jazz and Blues
    Festival, 16
Highland Village, 161
Hopewell Cape (Flowerpot
    Rocks), 38

Hubbards, 82

Ile-aux-Puces, 37
Ile Lamèque, 34–35
Ile Miscou, 35
Indian Harbour, 82
Indian Point, 142
Inn at Bay Fortune, 70
Inn Style Cooking Classes, 70
International Busker's
  Festival, 80
International Fox Museum
  and Hall of Fame, 46
International Festival of
  Baroque Music, 35
Inverness, 142
Inverness Miner's Museum,
  143
Iona, 161
Irish Festival on the
  Miramichi, 36
Irish Moss Interpretive Cen-
  tre, 50
Irving Nature Park, 13
Island Arts, 10
Island Chocolates, 45
Isle Madame, 167

Jacques Cartier Provincial
  Park, 51, 52
Joggins Fossil Centre, 134
Jost House, 162
Joy Laking Gallery, 132
Judique, 139
Julien's Pastry Shop, 85

Kedgwick, 26

Kedgwick Outdoor Recreation
  Centre, 26
Kejimkujik National Park, 92,
  124–26
Keltic Lodge, 154
Kidston Island Beach, 160
King's Head Inn, 18
King's Landing Historical Set-
  tlement, 17
Kouchibouguac National Park,
  36
K. R. Thompson, 86

La Bella Mona Lisa, 145
Lac Baker, 24
Lake George Provincial Park,
  19
La Sagouine, 37
L'Auberge Doucet, 146
Learn to Sail, 5
Leather Works, 155
Leavitts' Maple Tree Craft, 53
L'Église St.-Bernard, 112
Leif Erikson Picnic Park, 104
Le Motif, 147
Lennox Island, 55
LeNoir Forge Museum, 167
Leo's Cafe, 120
Le Pays de la Sagouine, 37
Les Jardins de La Republique,
  25
Le Village, 47
Lighthouse Artist Gallery and
  Chowder House, 75
Linden Cove Antiques, 60
Liscomb Lodge, 78
Little Harbour, 69

Little Narrows, 161
Liverpool, 89–91
Lobster Galley at Harbour House, 156
Lockeport, 94
Log Cabin Museum, 73
Lone Shieling, 151–52
Long Island, 114
Lookoff, 130
Lucy Maud Montgomery Heritage Museum, 59
Lunenburg, 82, 87–88
Lunenburg Academy, 87
Lunenburg craft festival, 87
Lunenburg Folk Harbour Festival, 87
Lynn Gorey's Craft Shop and Art Gallery, 154

Mabou, 139
Mabou Gaelic and Historical Society Museum, 140
Mabou Harbour Mouth, 141
Mabou Mines, 141
MacFarlane Woods Nature Reserve, 142
Machias Seal Island, 10
MacQueen's Bike Shop, 44, 62
Mahone Bay, 82, 86–87
Mahone Bay Settler's Museum, 86
Maitland, 131
Maitland Bridge, 125
Major Point Beach, 111
Malpeque Bay, 56
Malpeque Gardens, 57
Manan Island Inn and Spa, 10

Margaree River, 144
Margaree Salmon Museum, 144
Markland, 153
Matthew House Inn, 70
Mavilette Beach, 109
Mill River Golf Course, 54
Miminegash, 50
Minister's Island, 3
Mira River, 163
Mira River Provincial Park, 163
Miscou Lighthouse, 35
Moncton, 38
Mont Carmel Cultural Pioneer Village, 47
Morden, 128
Morrison's Pioneer Restaurant, 153
Mountain Gap Inn, 117
Mount Stewart, 64
Mrs. Profitt's Tea Room, 45
Mull, 140
Murray Harbour, 73
Musée Acadien, West Pubnico, 101
Musée de Cire d'Acadie, 34

National Exhibit Centre, 103
Naufrage, 66
Needles and Haystacks Bed and Breakfast, 65
New Brunswick's Legislative Assembly Building, 16
New Brunswick Botanical Garden, 25
New Denmark, 23

New Denmark Memorial Museum, 23
New London Bay, 59
New London Crafts and Antiques, 60
New London Seafood Restaurant, 60
Newman's, 119
Nicolas Denys Monument, 32
Nicolas Denys Museum, 166
North Cape, 51
North Head, 9
North Lake, 66
Norway, 51
Nova Scotia Folk Pottery, 84

Oak Island, 85
Oaklawn Farm Zoo, 127
Ocean Grill, 87
O'Dell Museum, 118
Odell Park, 17
Olde Village Inn, 115
Old Mira Trading Post, 163
Old Meeting House in Barrington, 99
Old Post Office, 119
Old Sow, 6
Orient Hotel, 45
Orwell Corner Historic Village, 75
Our Lady of Seven Sorrows Pioneers Shrine, 140
Ovens, The, 88
Overton, 104

Panmure Island, 72
Paquetville, 34

Parish Church of St. Simon and St. Jude, 52
Parrsboro, 133
Peggy's Cove, 82, 167
Perkins House, 89
Petit-Témis Interprovincial Park, 25
Pines Resort Hotel, 116
Piper's Cove, 161
Planter's Barracks Country Inn, 129
Pleasant Bay, 150
Pointe-Sapin, 36
Point Pleasant Park, 80
Point Prim Lighthouse, 75
Portaupique, 132
Port Hastings, 139
Port l'Hebert Pocket Wilderness, 93
Port Williams, 129
Prescott House, 129
Prince Edward Island, 42–44
Public Gardens, 80
Pubnico (West, Middle West and Lower West), 101

Quarterdeck Beachside Villas and Grill, 92
Queens County Museum, 91
Queensland, 82

Race Week, 85
Rafting, 132
Republique de Madawaska, 24
Restigouche Sam, 28
Rita MacNeil, 165
Rollo Bay fiddle festival, 66, 70

Rossignol Estate Winery, 74
Rossmount Inn, 4
Ross-Thomson House, 95

Sackville Waterfowl Park, 38
Saint John, 12–13
Saint John City Market, 13
Sandford, 108
Scarecrow Theatre, 145
Scots Bay, 130
Seabright, 82
Seal Cove, 11
Seaside Adjunct, 93
Seaweed Pie Café, 50
Shediac, 37
Shelburne, 94
Shelburne County Genealogical Research Centre, 97
Shelburne County Museum, 96
Sherbrooke, 78
Shippagan, 34
Shoreline Sweaters & Tyne Valley Studio, 56
Sir Andrew Macphail Homestead, 75
Sissibou Falls, 113
Smuggler's Cove, 110
South Lake, 67
South Shore, 82
Southwest Margaree, 143
Space Barn Museum, 108
Spinnakers' Landing, 46
Spinning Wheel Craft Shop, 60

St. Andrews, 64

St. Andrews by the Sea, 2–5
Stanley Bay Country Resort, 59
Stanley Bridge, 59
Stanley Bridge Studios, 59
Ste.-Anne du Ruisseau, 101
Ste.-Cécile, 35
St.-Léonard, 25
St. Margarets Bay, 82
St. Peter's, 165–67
St. Peter's Bay, 65
St. Peter's Canal, 166
St. Quentin, 26
St. Stephen, 2
Studio Gallery, 44
Sugarloaf, 28
Sunset Art Gallery, 147
Suttles and Seawinds, 86
Swallowtail Lighthouse, 11
Sydney, 162
Sydney and Louisbourg Railway Station Museum, 163

Tancook Islands, Big and Little, 83
Tattingstone, 131
Teazer, 86
Telegraph House, 160
Thomas Raddall Research Room, 91
Tidal Bore Rafting, 132
Tignish Heritage Inn and Hostel, 52–53
Town Point Cemetery, Chebogue, 101
Train Station Museum, 29
Twin Shores/Cabot Beach

Provincial Park, 58

Uisage Bann Falls, 161
Université Ste.-Anne, 110
Upper Clements Park, 117
Upper Clements Wildlife Park, 117

Valhalla Restaurant, 23
Victoria-by-the-Sea, 44–45
Victoria Playhouse, 44
Victoria Seaport Museum, 45
Village Vista Building, 60

Wallace MacAskill Museum, 167
Warp and Woof, 84
Washabuck Peninsula, 161
Waterloo Row, 15
Western festival, 26
Western Head, 91
West Point Lighthouse, 48

West Point Lighthouse Craft Guild, 50
Weymouth, 112
whale–watching cruises, 115
White Point Beach Lodge, 91
Whitman Inn, 125
Wind and Reef, 51
wooden boat festival, 86
Woodleigh, 57
Woodleigh Concerts on the Green, 57
World's Longest Covered Bridge, 19

Yarmouth, 92, 101–4
Yarmouth County Museum, 103
York-Sunbury Historical Society Museum, 14
Young Company, 64

ABOUT THE AUTHOR

Trudy Fong has worked as a journalist in Canada and in Southeast Asia. For a time she was a reporter for the *Hongkong Standard,* and then she turned to magazine writing. Before she settled into a steady job, she traveled around the world for three years with her husband Greg, during which time she visited and wrote about more than twenty-five countries. Trudy speaks several languages, including French, which was especially useful while researching this book. She lives in Nova Scotia with her husband and three sons.

Also of Interest from The Globe Pequot Press

Guide To Eastern Canada $18.95
     Toronto, Montreal, Ottawa, Ontario, and Quebec

Berlitz Discover Canada Guide $18.95
     Fully mapped itineraries, language tips, hotels, restaurants

Berlitz Travellers Guide to Canada $17.95
     Takes you beyond the usual tourist trappings

Berlitz Pocket Guide to Canada $10.95
     The most successful pocket-format travel guide series!

Woodall's 1996 Camping Guide for Canada $ 5.95
     All provinces

Available from your bookstore or directly from the publisher. For a free catalogue or to place an order, call toll free, 24 hours a day, 1-800-243-0495, or write to The Globe Pequot Press, P.O. Box 833, Old Saybrook, Connecticut 06475-0833.